THE ART OF
PERSUASION

Lars Hartveit

THE ART OF PERSUASION

A Study of Six Novels

Universitetsforlaget

Bergen – Oslo – Tromsø

© The Norwegian Research Council for Science and the Humanities 1977
(Norges almenvitenskapelige forskningsråd)
Section A.61.03.6T

ISBN 82-00-01668-4

Cover design by Per Syversen

Distribution offices:
NORWAY
Universitetsforlaget
Box 6589, Rodeløkka
Oslo 5

UNITED KINGDOM
Global Book Resources Ltd.
37, Queen Street
Henley on Thames
Oxon RG 9 1AJ

UNITED STATES and CANADA
Columbia University Press
136 South Broadway
Irvington-on-Hudson
New York 10533

Printed in Norway by
E. Høgfeldt Boktrykkeri A.s, Kristiansand S.

Contents

Introduction

I

The subject of this study is the art of persuasion, the strategies with which the novelist shapes and guides the reader's response to his work. The writer's persuasive urge is shown to seek two main channels, that of pattern and that of emphasis. The novel is presented as a shape or structure in which conventional elements like character, plot, setting, theme, and imagery are linked together by means of words. Emphasis is the way the author gives prominence to links in the sequence he has established or strands in the pattern he has woven. It also refers to point of view and types of commentary, and to verbal elements which control the reader's attitudes and views or determine the mood in which he reads the novel.

Each of the six chapters deals with a particular novel. The novels cover three centuries, but the historical aspect is of secondary importance, as they have not been chosen with reference to their chronological significance. In fact, I might say I have followed E. M. Forster's suggestion and gathered writers from different periods together in the same room and asked them to write their novels simultaneously.[1]

The choice is partly arbitrary, partly personal. These are novels I have lived with for a considerable length of time; some of them are indeed old friends. But I have also chosen them because they illustrate quite fully the novelist's persuasive range, and they emphasize that many aspects of the art of persuasion and its inherent problems are of a perennial character.

Each chapter focuses on a particular aspect of the art of persuasion, which is examined in relation to the main elements of fiction, in the context of language, design, and emphasis.

In my first chapter I discuss the didactic aspect of the art of persuasion as exemplified in Samuel Richardson's *Pamela*. This is followed by a chapter on George Eliot's use of a particular pattern of imagery – the door imagery – in *Silas Marner* to illustrate a particular social/moral view. In Chapter III Thomas Hardy's *The Mayor of Casterbridge* yields material for an analysis of the way a character may be given a particular persuasive function within the general framework of character, incident, and setting. The chapter on E. M. Forster's *A Passage to India* is concerned with the way design and accent produce a meaningful tension in the novel which is implicitly moral. Chapter V, on Graham Greene's *Brighton Rock,* deals with the impact of a predominantly religious view of man and his world on the various elements in the novel and the special problems of persuasion that such a view entails. Finally, in Chapter VI, Anthony Burgess is shown to have a dual persuasive aim in *A Clockwork Orange,* that of teaching a lesson and that of creating a self-contained world in which words have been stripped of their external moral values. A private language is developed which strains the limits of persuasion.

II

> ... the novelist is faced with formal problems different from those that confront other kinds of storyteller. ... Real life ... is not distinguished by unity, pattern and harmony. On the contrary, it is a heterogeneous, disorderly, indeterminate affair, full of loose ends and false starts and irrelevant details. How is the novelist to reconcile these two claims, how keep the delicate balance between the demands of life and art?[2]

These words by Lord David Cecil echo the traditional view of a dichotomy between the formlessness of life and the order or ordering power of art.[3] At first glance it may seem strange to include the novel as a genre in the category of art. Its intrinsic 'openness' and looseness seem to make it intractable to the demands of form, while these very qualities appear to make it eminently fitted to cope with life.[4] Yet Cecil is right in suggesting a fruitful tension between the pressure of chaotic life and the concern with order and coherence that is the hallmark of the novelist's craft. The novelist's awareness of the lack of meaning and pattern in the world around him frequently seems to spark off the process that turns base metal into gold. But in so doing he has also turned life into fiction, and begun to practise the art of lying. An isolationist view of the art of the novelist is apparent in certain twentieth-century writers who, despairing of rendering external reality, have turned to the art of expression, the verbal medium, and their own subjective experience.[5] But on closer inspection the impact of form on chaotic material is evident in any novel at any time, however well it succeeds in eluding shape or illuding shapelessness.

The links between the world of fiction and the external world — 'reality' — are many and complex, and often as elusive as the Scarlet

Pimpernel. The same elusiveness clings to the word reality. Does it refer to what is objectively 'there', like the chairs we sit in, and is it therefore linked with truth? Or is what is objectively 'there' only appearance, while true reality is hidden? Is reality a framework of concepts that can be perceived — intuitively or intellectually? These and many similar questions have teased philosophers and religious thinkers from time immemorial. No agreement has been reached. No wonder terms like 'reality', 'real', and 'realism' are dangerously slippery; yet they are amazingly alive,[6] perhaps because they are so controversial.

The attitude to reality revealed in a novel may therefore vary a great deal. The author may feel that he is imitating the reality he perceives around him, while finding himself entangled in the time-honoured argument about the status of the literary work, the issue of autonomy versus imitation. According to Graham Hough 'literature creates fictitious objects', the products of 'free invention on the one hand and imitation on the other ...'[7] The matter is further complicated as the novelist creates images of reality, representing accuracy of detail, the recorder's states of feeling, and standing for something that may be both manifold and amorphous. Similarly, character and action may reflect the world of mortals and the author's feelings about this world, but they, too, represent something that is far too comprehensive to be encompassed within the narrow confines of the world of fiction. At the same time all these elements are embedded in language — a dimension that is lacking in the world of objects and which in the human world is only one of a number of ordering media.

The circumstance that the world of the novel is the product of impulses from reality, of the ordering power of the author's imagination, and of his command of language creates the effect of 'life and pattern' which Arnold Kettle feels characterizes the novel form. He seems to use 'pattern' in two senses, one relating to the author's vision of 'significance', that is perception of meaning and order in life, the other to 'form'.[8]

'Life' and 'form' focus our attention on two important aspects of the novelist's craft. One is his function as creator and 'fashioner'. He is a 'maker', but he also possesses 'the Daedalian faculty for selection and cunning manipulation...'[9] His other function is that of showing up the pattern of life, its meaning and inherent values. Even when he is an 'anti-visionary', imbued with the belief that existence is meaningless, the idea of literary form seems to insist on a pattern.

The relative emphasis on life and pattern has varied down through the ages. The eighteenth-century novelist wrote so as to teach and delight, i.e. he concerned himself with the business of human conduct, but presented his instruction in a pleasing form. In the nineteenth century, pattern appears to have been subordinated to life, and being true to life was considered the novelist's prime duty. With the rise of the modernist or anti-realistic novel in the 1920s the situation is reversed: now pattern is the prime concern of writer as well as critic.

There are signs at present that critical opinion is veering towards a more balanced view of life and pattern in relation to the novel. Victorian and earlier fiction is being rediscovered. Increasing importance is attached to traditional elements in the novel such as story, plot, character, and incident. Thus Barbara Hardy stresses that the 'novel holds us by its story and informs us by its moral argument, but it moves us by its individual presences and moments ...'[10] Leading critics unashamedly confess to their realist predilections.[11] On the other hand, there are also signs that another pattern phase is on its way: the novel is seen to constitute a world that resembles external reality, but is an autonomous unit or structure.[12]

The present work is concerned with the pattern presented by six novels, chosen from three centuries of English fiction. The gulf between *Pamela* and *A Clockwork Orange* may seem unbridgeable, yet they share a number of basic problems, which confronted their authors as well as their readers. One is related to the narrative method used, that of the first person narrator. Another is the conflict between the demands of form and the pressure of the underlying moral vision, the author's 'message'.

The novels share a common concern with the human predicament. Man is equipped with the means of communication and feels intensely the need for meaningful contact with his fellow human beings, but he finds himself lonely, isolated, incapable of establishing relationships based on trust and loyalty. The worlds depicted in these novels display varying degrees of indifference or hostility towards the individual. This hostility may in some cases extend to the whole universe. Also, in all the novels the urge for form is combined with an urge to tame the mysterious and obscure through language. This is revealed in a tendency to repeat words and details that may seem trivial, but that assume significance because they are forever being hammered into the reader's consciousness.

The author's power over the reader is intimately linked with his skill in using words. His success as a novelist depends on his ability to achieve verbal contact with his readers. David Lodge traces the complex nature of the relationship between writing and reading novels:

... in literary discourse, the writer discovers what he has to say in the process of saying it, and the reader discovers what is said in responding to the way it is said. In the reading of literature, therefore, the expressive, the cognitive, and the affective are inextricably mingled. The writer expresses what he knows by affecting the reader; the reader knows what is expressed by being receptive to affects. The medium of this process is language.[13]

10

The importance of language as the one and only means of communication between author and reader is of course demonstrated in every novel. The emphasis on 'the expressive, the cognitive, and the affective', varies however. The novel covers a wide range of 'worlds', from the everyday to the apocalyptic. But the novelist always needs to impose upon the reader through language. His skill in exploiting the resources of language to persuade the reader to suspend his disbelief is the final test of his skill as fabulator.

An important aspect of the present work is the relationship between author–work–reader. When reading a novel, we are entirely at the author's mercy. This is true in the obvious sense that he is the omnipotent creator, to whom our thanks are due. The reader may be able to influence him – the taste of the reading public after all determines the sales of his books. But all the same his pen is the key to the world his book offers, and we cannot change this world once it has been created. The author is also in innumerable ways our guide, who

signpost[s] the way for the alert and sensitive reader, unobtrusively drawing attention to the shaping process itself by deliberate heightenings and intensifications of style, or by some other means: dramatized incident, interior monologue, recurrent image, or direct comment.[14]

The reader's function in the world of the novel is hard to assess. In eighteenth-century and Victorian fiction he is often palpably present because the author tends to address him over the heads of his characters. This is unusual in modern fiction, although Anthony Burgess makes use of the convention in *A Clockwork Orange*. It seems nevertheless obvious that a 'fictitious' reader is present, at least in the author's mind, and we have just seen how important Lodge considers him to be. Lodge's view is close to that of Wolfgang Iser, who says that although the novel 'presents no real objects, it nevertheless establishes its reality by the reader's participation and by the reader's response.'[15] In other words, the world of the novel only becomes 'real' when it is related, in the reader's consciousness, to the external world.

The reader is, in the last resort, the author's touchstone. It is his reception of the work that determines its fate. Coleridge emphasized the importance of the reader's 'willing suspension of disbelief' when confronted with supernatural elements. The question of belief is undoubtedly important in the reading process, although Scholes and Kellogg may be right in assuming that 'the reality of fiction . . . depends on the reader's partial belief and partial disbelief.'[16] After all Coleridge stresses that the suspension of disbelief is 'willing', in other words a deliberate act or tacit agreement. Scholes and Kellogg go as far as seeing the reader as not merely the author's 'accessory', but also his 'accomplice.'[17] Loofbourow suggests two ways in which a reader may respond to the 'realisms' the author has created. He may seek to " 'identify' " with them, or he may find 'pleasure' in the 'recognition of the artist's imitative skill . . .'[18] The author is the reader's guide, but the reader is also a critical intelligence, a discoverer.[19] Neither pattern nor life may be immediately discernible, but they become so in the course of the reading process, which depends on critical (and creative) surrender to the world 'we usually enter as a foreign visitor . . .'[20]

Words like 'guide' and 'signpost' indicate an important function of the novelist: he practises 'the art of persuasion',[21] which, according to Wayne C. Booth, is 'the art of communicating with readers . . . to impose his fictional world upon [them].'[22] The writer obviously exploits all his resources to do this, and the structure as well as the texture of his book may enhance its persuasive power. Also, he may, perhaps without knowing it, release certain responses in the reader that are 'conventional' in that they belong to their common cultural heritage. The range is wide, stretching from the Bible and inherited moral and religious patterns to the bestseller and its reliance upon certain character types, plot elements and clichés. An interesting ironical effect may be achieved by pitting the reader's critical sense against the stock response displayed by the character(s). On the other hand, a didactically inclined writer may play on traditional contrasts and responses. *Pamela* is a case in point. The interest and value of this novel depend largely on the way we are made to respond to the tension displayed between conventional roles that accentuate the novel's moral pattern, and the characters' (above all the heroine's) claims as individuals in their own right. These contrasting interests are felt in all the novels discussed. The problem may be inherent in the novel form itself, which, as mentioned above, presents characters who are both 'individuals' and therefore 'particulars', and representatives, typifying mankind as a whole.

Point of view, as a writer like Wayne C. Booth has shown, is an important means of controlling the reader's response. Karl Kroeber draws attention to 'its function as an indicator of the novelist's relation, or . . . his conception of his relation, to his readers.'[23] In a previous work I have discussed the way point of view may be used to establish a relationship of varying distance between author and character.[24] The persuasive element in fiction has attracted increasing attention since Booth published *The Rhetoric of Fiction* in 1961. Evidence of such a trend may be found in Malcolm Bradbury's *Possibilities*, notably in his essay on 'The Novel and Its Poetics'[25] and in a number of essays in John Halperin's collection of essays on *The Theory of the Novel.*[26] In the present study point of view is regarded as a major means of controlling the reader's response. All the novels discussed furnish evidence of such a function, but the problem receives most attention in the chapters on

12

A Passage to India and *Brighton Rock*. In the former, point of view is the accent at the heart of the design, in the latter it is the instrument which relates the metaphysical sphere to that of ordinary mortals.

CHAPTER I

Samuel Richardson, *Pamela* I. The Impact of Moral Exemplum: The Dilemma of the Didactic Writer

Ian Watt, in *The Rise of the Novel*, carefully documents the intricate links between *Pamela* and the age to which it belongs. He shows how the expectations of the reader of romances and devotional literature are both exploited and modified to fit and exemplify the Puritan concept of marriage and sexual relationship.[1] *Pamela* is steeped in the traditional language of moral instruction, yet it manages to transcend the inherent limitations.

From start to finish *Pamela* poses a fundamental problem: how can the didactic writer make his wish to teach and instruct conform with the 'rights' of his heroine as an 'independent' fictitious character? The epistolary form accentuates the problem rather than solves it. Pamela's sigh at the outset of her imprisonment that 'there is nothing so hard to be known as the heart of man . . .' (p. 103),[2] refers to her private experience of distress, but at the same time it is a general moral observation.

The words, however, seem personal rather than 'public' owing to the crisis that wrung them from her. At the nadir of her fortunes Pamela has discovered that no one can be trusted, not even John Arnold, B.'s footman, whom she had trusted with her letters to her parents. He, too, has been used against her.

Pamela's reflection shows that she has come a long way since, as a fifteen–year–old girl, she found herself deprived of the guidance and protection her mistress had afforded her. In her first letter after Lady B.'s death Pamela is full of confident hopes about her future on the estate. B. had promised her mother to look after the young girl and her fellow servants, solemnly declaring, ' "I will take care of you all, my good maidens" ' (p. 1). It obviously does not occur to Pamela to suspect B.'s motives when he is kind and generous to her.[3] It is her father, representing religion, morality, and worldly experience, who first warns her that a trap may be prepared to catch her 'jewel', her virtue.[4] Characteristically, he writes about 'design' where she had merely seen goodness, and he is particularly anxious that her gratitude should not blind her to the danger of temptation. At the same time he emphasizes the superior value of virtue to 'riches' or 'any worldly convenience', affirming trust 'in God's goodness' as the only reliable basis for happiness in this life and the next (pp. 3–4).

Pamela is at first puzzled. There is even a hint of displeasure at her father's letter, because 'it has made [her] heart, which was overflowing with gratitude for [her] master's goodness, suspicious and fearful . . .' (p. 4). The letter (III) contains the first example of one of Pamela's characteristic features, her tendency to argue and reason. In the first line she complains that her parents' letter has 'filled [her] with trouble.' Then she expresses the hope that she will 'never find him [B.] act unworthy of his character . . .' This is followed by an attempt to convince herself and her parents of the unlikelihood that the young squire would behave badly towards her, 'for what could he get by ruining such a young poor creature . . .?' She establishes a logic of property, wealth, and rank, to which she clings throughout. Subsequent events prove that her logic gives her a false sense of security, but she does not really ever admit that she is wrong. Although forced by circumstances to grant that her logic is not self-evident, she is convinced that the truth it contains will eventually be discovered and accepted by the parties concerned.

After blaming her parents for not trusting their own daughter, she assures them,

. . . I never will do any thing that shall bring your gray hairs with sorrow to the grave. I will die a thousand deaths rather than be dishonest any way (p. 4).

Although she has lived above her station for some time, she is their *dutiful daughter* who 'can be content with rags, poverty, and bread and water, and will embrace them, rather than forfeit [her] good name, let who will be the tempter' (p. 4).

Because Pamela has trusted her master so implicitly, she feels she has been deceived and betrayed when he makes his first attempt upon her. She has praised his goodness and even raised him to angelic heights, perhaps to refute her parents' suspicion. But reporting the disaster that has overtaken her world of trust and bliss, she emphasizes the enormity of the event by apostrophizing him as 'this angel of a master! this fine gentleman! this gracious benefactor to your poor Pamela!' (p. 10). She might have used these words about B. before the event, in full earnest, but his fall from grace has turned them into invectives. She has been disillusioned, but her words allude to the pedestal of admiration from which he has fallen and which she can never quite forget.

Pamela is at times blamed for her suspiciousness. Thus Mark Kinkead-Weekes refers to 'the damaging suspiciousness which blinds her to the complexity of other people.'[5] B. criticizes her for her lack of trust during the period between his last attempt and their marriage. But considering her long ordeal it seems quite reasonable that she should find it difficult to get over the anxiety and suspiciousness that experience has taught her.

Circumspection and caution seem the inevitable responses of an intelligent mind left to itself and its own resources. *Pamela* explores the potentialities of the individual when faced with apparently overwhelming difficulties. The initial letters also show that a consequence of B.'s fall is Pamela's fall from innocent trustfulness. It is part of the basic paradox of the novel that in order to safeguard innocence and virtue, trustfulness must be qualified by caution, the fruit of experience, which can only be gained in a world which endangers virtue. On the other hand, it is also true that Pamela has to conquer the general suspiciousness which circumstances have fostered in her before she can be admitted to the bliss and happiness which her marriage to B. has in store for her.[6] In a sense she is readmitted to the land of innocence that she inhabited at the outset.

Despite B.'s numerous attacks, Pamela's innocence is preserved, as is B.'s. After their marriage they journey back into their Bedfordshire Eden, welcomed by grateful servants, including John. A ceremonial restoration of trust takes place as part of the general celebrations. The servants are forgiven for their plotting; gifts are showered on them; and there is a final emphasis on the benevolent landlord and his virtuous lady, bent on doing good. Virtue has been rewarded, as the sub-title of the novel suggests, and a heart free of care and suspicion is part of the reward.

Critics have tended to dwell on the apparent conflict between Richardson's didactic aim and his true gift as a novelist of character. Pamela, it is claimed, achieves life and individuality despite the author's intention to set her up as an example to the maidservants of England.[7] One is undoubtedly continually made aware of 'the disparity between the conventional and the actual attitudes of the lovers . . .'[8] This disparity is above all felt in the contrast between Pamela as an exemplary character and Pamela as a character in her own right. In moments of crisis she is shown to possess integrity and resources of speech and temperament that transform her into an autonomous character. On the other hand, the requirement that she should be a light to her readers, and the impact of milieu and of prevalent moral and religious norms are so inextricably interwoven with character, temperament, and manners that it is very difficult to distinguish clearly between the two Pamelas.

Sincerity is therefore a serious problem in *Pamela*. Is the attitude displayed merely outward show, or does it spring from conviction? Does the idiom used reflect genuine feeling, or does it only pay lip service to the conventional lessons taught by parents and superiors? The epistolary form complicates the problem. There is no commentator to evaluate

Pamela's views and conduct. The author obviously draws on the traditional types of pious and moral literature, like conduct books, sermons, and tracts,[9] which provided reading matter for Pamela as well as models of behaviour. The pose and the lesson-taught approach are encouraged. Knowledge of 'the heart of man', including the heroine's own heart, involves exploration and exposure of hidden areas of the mind. But we are only given inadvertent glimpses. 'For Richardson', David Daiches remarks, 'all the tests of life are public . . . There is no private wrestling with one's soul or with the devil here . . . no purely private anguish . . .'[10]

The letter form suggests that what may originally have been private has been publicized, however limited the audience. Daiches compares the epistolary technique with 'the soliloquy in drama and the so-called stream of consciousness technique in modern fiction. We are brought immediately and directly into the consciousness of the character.'[11] The soliloquy, however, externalizes internal conflict, often expressing it in the formal language of argument. Pamela tends to do this in her letters. But the stream of consciousness technique aims at conveying the fluidity and formlessness of inarticulate thought, the way the conscious and subconscious flow into each other ceaselessly, prior to speech and logical form, without beginning or end. Pamela's letters, on the other hand, focus attention on the moment when conflicting emotions come to the surface and the previous fluidity congeals in the fixed form of formal language.

Critics like McKillop and Watt stress the 'writing to the moment' approach to experience which Richardson felt the epistolary method afforded. Watt feels that

the use of the epistolary method impels the writer towards producing something that may pass for the spontaneous transcription of the subjective reactions of the protagonists to the events as they occur . . .[12]

Pamela's letters bring us 'extremely close to [her] inner consciousness . . .'[13] McKillop draws attention to the way the epistolary method

gives the reader a continuous and cumulative impression of living through the experience . . . here we have the close linking of memory and current impression with anticipation of what is to come . . . a future emerging directly from the specious present . . .[14]

The immediacy mentioned by Watt is partly achieved by means of dialogue – incidents tend to be dramatically rendered. The sense of anticipation that McKillop writes about recurs throughout the novel, preceding both dreadful and joyful events. It contributes to the prevailing atmosphere of an unavoidable fate. The ways of Providence may be inscrutable, but are felt to play an active part in the lives of the characters, in keeping with orthodox Puritanical teaching. During Pa-

17

mela's prolonged agony the sense of imminent danger is a major cause of the anxiety and insecurity surrounding her trials.

On the other hand, it is evident that however quickly Pamela trips into her closet to record the event, it is already past when she picks up her pen; the experience is complete. The reader is presented with her finished version of it. The immediacy is therefore qualified by a certain finality. The future may be uncertain, but the present has been stripped of some of its terror because it is already past.

Pamela's letters are not only nearly-on-the-spot records of her trials; they also contain her reactions to the events. She evaluates, judges, reflects, at the same time revealing her feelings and states of mind as a result of the vicissitudes she records. When she tells Lady Davers that her letters should be considered 'as the naked sentiments of [her] heart . . .' (p. 412), she is not implying that they are private and therefore inaccessible to the world. She means that she did not have readers like Lady Davers in mind when she wrote them. She is anxious to establish her sincerity: her letters faithfully express her feelings and views at the time of her suffering. Also, 'sentiments' indicate the completion of her emotional experience at the various stages of her ordeal; it has been included in the heroine's moral vocabulary.

The passage that records John Arnold's treachery and Pamela's discovery of the intractability of 'the heart of man' illustrates the way the epistolary method can unite immediacy and afterthought. John's letter is first copied and made to speak for itself. Her own words anticipate her parents' reaction and record her own: '. . . I make no doubt your hair will stand on end as mine does!' (p. 102). Her plain, colloquial language – common usage as well as Pamela's own idiom – stresses the shock she experienced at the man's treachery. This is Pamela's usual way of rendering spontaneous experience. Then follows a general reflection, 'O the deceitfulness of the heart of men!' (p. 102). John's betrayal of her is the final link in a long chain of evidence that causes her to pass the verdict of 'deceitfulness' on men in general. Her own bitter experience bears out what she has read and been taught, releasing moral sentiment.

The third stage in the process started by John's letter is a sort of mental court case against the offender, articulated in Pamela's letter and thus externalized. The extent of John's treachery and deceitfulness is shown up:

This John, that I took to be the honestest of men; that you took for the same; that was always praising you to me, and me to you, and for nothing so much as for our *honest* hearts; this *very* fellow was all the while a vile hypocrite, and a perfidious wretch, and helping to carry on my ruin (pp. 102-3).

The condemnatory force of the indictment at the end of the quotation is heightened by the reader's having been taken step by step through

John's past relationship with Pamela and her family. The recapitulation of his words of praise for them and their trust in him lends force to her damning charge of hypocrisy and perfidy.

She is now moved to make her observation about the 'heart of man'. Her eyes have been opened, and she is utterly shocked to find '[t]hat power and riches never want tools to promote their vilest ends . . .' (p. 103). We have, however, moved a long way from spontaneous experience. Pamela is now in her closet, reflecting on what has happened and formulating moral sentiments of general relevance. She no doubt emerges from the experience 'a wiser but a sadder' person, but she is bent on generalizing from her personal experience to the common human lot.

Pamela's general verdicts and observations on human nature are followed by rather an anticlimax. She resolves to keep John's 'wickedness secret'. He 'seems to have great remorse . . .', and Pamela is therefore encouraged to 'pity the poor wretch' (p. 103), and hopes to lead him to a state of 'penitence'. Her language is peppered with conventional religious-moral idioms: pity, penitence, forgiveness. But, characteristically, Pamela adds a humanising touch. She is not only a saintly Christian, she is also a maiden in distress who has vested interests in John's fall: '. . . I will encourage his penitence', she says, 'for I may possibly make some discoveries by it' (p. 103).

Pamela is an indefatigable plotter, which from time to time exposes her to accusations of deceit and hypocrisy. On this occasion her words serve to remove her from the pinnacle of piousness and show up her human weakness — or strength. Pamela is always circumspect and her presence of mind never fails her. Besieged by her master and his helpers, she lives after all in a state of war. In such a context people are either friends or foes, and treason is a capital offence. She takes due heed of John's warning that her 'ruin has been long hatching' (p. 103), and immediately starts working on poor Mr. Williams, the young clergyman on the estate.

During the rest of her entry for 'the fifth Day of [her] Bondage and Misery' she reflects in a kind of soliloquy on the source of John's corruption, and ponders the puzzling question of why B. should 'carry on a plot, to ruin a poor creature, who never did him any harm, nor wished him any . . .' (p. 103). She displays her skill in logical reasoning. This may at times lead her astray and blind her to the real issues, but it also reveals her firm grasp on value and verbal command. Her apparently naive questions suggest that she has been imprisoned in a world of upside-down values:

John had *some* inducement; for he hoped to please his master . . . But what inducement has my *master* . . . If he loves me . . . must he therefore lay traps for me, to ruin me . . .? I cannot imagine what good the undoing of such a poor creature as

I can procure him. — To be sure I am a very worthless body. People say I am handsome; but if I was so, should not a gentleman prefer an honest servant to a guilty harlot? And must he be *more* earnest to seduce me, because I dread to be seduced, and would rather lose my life than my honesty (pp. 103–4).

The passage highlights the stock situation of the first half of *Pamela* — virtue resisting the attempts of the wicked seducer. It is fraught with moral implications, apparent in the sentiments expressed and in the contrasts on which Pamela dwells. But we are also given a close-up of the contradictory thoughts and impulses which run through her mind at this critical moment. Her questions and reflections suggest that she is playing hide-and-seek with her own heart.

There is some evidence of posing in the above passage, particularly when she alludes to what people say about her beauty. One may wonder at times if she is quite so artless as her questions imply. There are also some traces of a hidden fascination with the idea of seduction and prostitution, which she rejects on the surface with such horror. Our main impression, however, is one of genuine bewilderment. Here, as on most occasions when she is faced with a problematic situation, Pamela falls back on her own reason and wit, her main weapons in her verbal duels with B. The quotation illustrates her tendency to speak in antithetic contrasts: wicked master–innocent virtue; honest servant–harlot; love–trap; worthless–(by implication) invaluable. Perhaps without knowing it, she diagnoses the perverse nature of B.'s fascination with her: it is her resistance, her firm belief that her virtue is more valuable than her life, that inflames his desire to conquer her.

The fondness for a rhetorical ordering of contrasts displayed throughout the novel corresponds to a distribution of roles and attitudes that also provides antithetic patterns. The passage just quoted indicates some of them. There are, first of all, the roles of master and servant and the relationship between them. The novel raises the related problem of the extent of the master's influence and the servant's duties towards his/her master. Implied is the contrast between the good and the bad master. Pamela's reflections on 'the fifth Day of [her] Bondage' and the context in which they occur set her up as a maiden in distress, kept imprisoned by her persecuting cruel master. This is a fairytale or romance motif,[15] but Richardson has moved it into an eighteenth-century rural setting. The motif of the pure maiden threatened by her rake of a master is superimposed on the romance motif. There are also reverberations of legends about saintly women exposed to the torments of this world. Linked with these motifs is that of the corruption of the innocent country girl. The underlying anxiety and terror are stressed by allusions to the giant of the fairytale and the eternal tempter of the Christian religion.

The roles suggested here, together with a number of others, and the typical responses and attitudes they imply, constitute the moral and religious conventions that provide the framework for Pamela and the other characters in the novel. These roles determine the action of the novel, the nature of the relationships that are established, the characters' attitudes to each other, and the language they speak. Clichés and stock responses are particularly interesting because they both spring from and support his framework. Recurrent use of particular words and phrases is an important means of establishing a role or contrasting roles. Such phrases often show the automatic way in which a character reacts when he represents a role or is confronted with one. They may also illustrate how even clichés may at times strike fire and become meaningful, particularly at moments of crisis.

Right from the first letter a set of social roles are established that dominate the pattern of the novel. McKillop demonstrates the importance of the social framework within which the heroine asserts herself.[16] The accuracy of the picture we are given of eighteenth-century society is discussed by Ian Watt and Diana Spearman. The latter is sceptical about attempts to see Richardson's novels as accurate reflections of the society to which he belonged.[17] William M. Sale warns us that it may be useful to 'say that Richardson reflects his age . . . but if it results in setting him apart from his age, we may fail to see that his age was, among other things, Richardson and his fiction.'[18]

The problem of accuracy of social portrayal[19] is relevant to our discussion mainly with regard to the author's use of social roles and concepts he either found in the society of his age or would have liked to find there. In a novel that aims at instruction and tries to set up examples for its readers, there is inevitably a mixture of realism and idealism. The reader is clearly meant to find features that relate the novel to his own everyday world, but he is also provided with a model which, if it were imitated, would improve the reality he knows. Besides, Richardson's tendency to pattern and stylize by singling out contrasting elements and arranging them in recurrent combinations, removes the world of his novel from the far more diffuse world which it may be said to reflect.

The opening letters illustrate this simplifying and ordering process. Pamela assumes her position as servant, admittedly of a somewhat superior kind. She defines her mistress's position as benevolent protectress. At the opposite end of the social scale is her parents' humble station. The concept of degree is thus introduced, and its importance made clear. It involves respect for one's social superiors. The system is both static and dynamic. Pamela was born into a humble station, but her mistress's benevolence has already raised her to a higher. It is clear that one who has the power to exalt another, of low degree, to a higher station is his/her social superior.

21

In the first letter we are told how Lady B. had given Pamela a train-ing which 'made ... [her] qualified above [her] degree ...' (p. 1). B. shows the same benevolence as his mother. To begin with, as we have seen, he acts the part of a kind and generous landlord with great propriety. Pamela, on her part, responds appropriately, with gratitude and obedience. B. is shown as the source of power and wealth in this little community, showering gold, silver, and clothes on his happy sub-ject, Pamela. He is seen as goodness personified. 'O how amiable a thing is doing good', sighs Pamela, 'It is all I envy great folks for.' (p. 7). 'Doing good', that is acting one's part as benevolent patriarch, is the privilege and responsibility of those of high degree.[20] They are all kings in their little domains, and they automatically release a response of obedience and gratitude.

This is the way Pamela has been taught to respond to her master, and the way she wants to respond. But when B. makes attempts on her virtue, she sees him not only as a fallen angel, but also as one who has violated the conventions of his social class, and she speaks and be-haves accordingly. B. is reduced to a tyrant. He sticks to his position and demands submission in sexual as well as social matters. He seems to fall back upon the ancient rights of the feudal lord. Pamela, how-ever, makes it quite clear that when the social system is exploited in such a way that her role clashes with her faith and conscience, she con-siders herself released from her bond of obedience.[21] She defends her-self with great courage, never confusing the issues, and in the end emerges victorious.

Pamela may at first glance seem a rebel. But she is a rebel in a very limited sense. She rejects B.'s interpretation of the rights of the master and his superior position in all contexts. She also rejects his role as generous giver when the price she has to pay is her own integrity, i.e. her virtue. Neither is she prepared to accept his set of values according to which her 'honesty' is a trifle and his attempts on her virtue harm-less. Pamela rebels against an outmoded social system in which the person of a mean servant girl is of no consequence. She asserts the individual's right to personal integrity. The whole emphasis in *Pamela* is on individualism[22] and, up to a point, on the rights of the individual.

But Pamela is also extremely conservative within the system to which she belongs. She sees B.'s behaviour towards her as a fall from social eminence; he has demeaned himself. We have seen how puzzled she is at the motives for his behaviour: ' "... if he can stoop to such a poor girl as me," ' Pamela asks Mrs. Jervis, ' "... what can it be *for*?" ' (p. 29). She feels that he has undermined the system of degree by stooping to her. His misdemeanour releases her tongue, words being indeed her main means of defence. She assumes the role of accuser as well as defender, asking B. sternly, ' "Let me ask you, Sir, if you think this becomes your fine clothes, and a master's station?'" (p. 56). As early as his first attempt, she makes one of her most essential points. When he argues that he has done her no harm, she retorts,

'Yes, Sir ... the greatest harm in the world: you have taught me to forget myself, and what belongs to me, and have lessened the distance that fortune has made between us, by demeaning yourself, to be so free to a poor servant' (p. 12).

Her accusation plays on the apparently absolute polarities of her social system — B.'s high position, her lowliness. The kind of link B. is contemplating, in addition to its moral and religious inadmissibility, is a breach of social decorum.

In all her debates with B. Pamela sticks to the existing social order and uses it as a weapon against his attempts. Pamela may ceremonially (or instinctively) show her submission to her master by falling on her knees in an attitude of prayer for mercy, but her words define the limits of her obedience:[23] '"For heaven's sake ... pity a poor creature, that knows nothing of her duty, but how to cherish her virtue and good name!"' (p. 19). B. asks, '"Is it not one part of honesty to be dutiful and grateful to your master..."', but as usual, Pamela has an answer ready which presents her interpretation of her duties to her master: '"Indeed, Sir ... it is impossible I should be ungrateful to your honour, or disobedient ... but when your commands are contrary to that first duty which shall ever be the principle of my life"' (p. 19).

Ian Watt draws attention to the way B.'s 'courtship ... involves a struggle, not only between two individuals, but between two opposed conceptions of sex and marriage held by different social classes...'[24] This basic disagreement is seen in B.'s continuous efforts to minimize what he is trying to do by using phrases like 'no harm' about his intentions and 'foolish' about her resistance. He is also for ever trying to tempt her with money and riches, the standard resort of the rich young man. Pamela's attitude is revealed in her steadfast refusal to sell her virtue. It is a little unfair to charge her with a commercial attitude to her virtue[25] – it is her master who thinks of Pamela's virtue as a commodity that money can buy.

Pamela's real commodity, apart from her moral-religious conviction, is lack of money – her 'property' is absolute poverty. She continually asserts her parents' honest poverty in defiance of the social and moral corruption she has seen in higher stations. Poverty is claimed to be devoid of the snares and temptations that beset the rich. At the height of her distress she assures B., '"... all I desire is, to be permitted to return to my native meanness unviolated. ... my beloved poverty"' (pp. 167–8). She uses this way of life as a weapon against her tormentor, but it also appears to her as a pastoral haven of bliss and contentment.

Pamela writes about her parents' 'poor, but happy abode . . .', and dreams of her father's 'cot' (p. 70).

However, extreme poverty is also the grim reality that faces her on her departure from B.'s estate. She wonders how she will fare, fully aware that her training will be of little use to her, ' ". . . it had been better to have been brought up to hard labour . . ." ' (p. 66). There is a hint that Pamela would feel it degrading to return to her social origins. However, she comforts herself with her pastoral dream, which makes the idea of banishment more palatable:

'Bread and water I can live upon with content. Water I shall get any where; and if I can't get bread, I will live, like a bird in winter, upon hips and haws, and at other times upon pig-nuts, potatoes, or turnips' (p. 66).

The very real social dilemma in which Pamela finds herself is resolved by her grim prospects' becoming turned into a fairytale.

Pamela's pastoral dream serves two purposes. It satisfies the didactic aim by representing the Puritanical ideal of frugality and contentment. For Pamela it is a source of comfort in what to her is harsh reality, a hidden reserve from which she can draw courage and strength.

Pamela combines the role of accuser, who takes her stand on the concept of social degree, with that of preacher, who upholds the social doctrine to which she clings. Thus she asserts the distance between servant and master: ' ". . . what proposals can one in your high station have to make to one in my low degree!" ' (p. 120). Again and again she puts forward this assertion of absolute distance so that it becomes part of her idiom. On the other hand, high society imagery, belonging to the common stock of ordinary phrases on which Pamela draws, acquires peculiar significance in her situation. A remark like '. . . what can the abject poor do against the mighty rich, when they are determined to oppress?' (p. 83), rather trite though it is, is redeemed by the ordeal that gave rise to it. She seems to speak not only for herself, but for all the poor and oppressed. At the same time, she indirectly asserts her determination not to be intimidated. On another occasion she challenges B.'s authority in 'royal language': ' "But, O Sir! my *soul* is of equal importance with the soul of a princess, though my quality is inferior to that of the meanest slave" ' (p. 137). Later she declares that her ' "virtue is as dear to [her] as if [she] was of the highest quality . . ." ' (p. 190).

Pamela's royal imagery is rooted in common usage, at the same time demonstrating her fondness for antithetic contrasts and her aptitude for the memorable phrase. She speaks with the tongue of moral earnestness, but her words acquire emotional intensity from her own personal crisis.

Pamela reveals an ambiguous attitude to social degree. She defies the social pattern by putting herself, when her soul is at stake, on a level with the highest in the land. But her emphasis on the polarity of high and low also shows how deeply rooted such a division is in her nature and temperament. Faced with eternity, there is no difference between 'the richest of princes, and the poorest of beggars ...' (p. 229), but the 'chain of being' is, in the human community, a system of degrees.

Pamela's tendency to exalt herself to the level of princes when her virtue is in danger is balanced by an equally strong tendency to prostrate herself, thus annihilating her own social importance. She achieves this effect by associating herself with the bottom of the social scale. B., on the other hand, is seen as one of the high, even included among the royal few. His fall is the greater because he has the makings of a royal, even heavenly potentate. These extremes are well brought out in a scene towards the end of Pamela's trials, in which she is taken to task for trying to run away:

> He put on a stern and majestic air; and he can look very majestic when he pleases. 'Well, perverse Pamela, ungrateful runaway,' ... I could not speak; but throwing myself on the floor, hid my face, and was ready to die with grief and apprehension. – He said, 'Well may you hide your face! well may you be ashamed to see me, vile forward one as you are!' I sobbed, and wept, but could not speak. And he let me lie, and went to the door, and called Mrs. Jewkes. 'There,' said he, 'take up that fallen angel! ... The little hypocrite prostrates herself thus, in hopes to move my weakness in her favour, and that I'll raise her from the floor myself. But I shall not touch her' (p. 159).

We must bear in mind that we are only given Pamela's version of what happened. The scene is seen through Pamela's eyes. But the reader is able to see elements of which the protagonist is obviously unaware. Undoubtedly B. humiliates her with a touch of sadistic pleasure; he enjoys seeing her writhing on the floor. But Pamela, too, in a way enjoys the situation. B. has always appeared majestic to her. As long as he left her virtue alone, she enjoyed feeling that she was ruled by him and dependent on his favour and goodness. On this and other occasions there is a touch of religious awe in her attitude of prostration.

Pamela indicates the manner in which the eighteenth-century reader would be expected to assume the existence of a social pattern that had been instituted by Providence. Through his 'station' B. embodies the principle of paternal authority, Pamela as a servant maid is expected to submit to the principle of deferential obedience. The medieval concept of the chain of being – a basic metaphor in Pope's *Essay on Man* – survives in eighteenth-century social and religious thinking. There is a lingering emphasis on the underlying divine order or plan, and the paternal wisdom of Providence.[26]

The passage just quoted starts the process of metamorphosis that Pamela undergoes in the second half of the novel. Exaltation is perhaps a better word for what happens to her: she is raised from her lowliness to B.'s dizzying height. From the moment she has conquered her suspiciousness and he has offered to marry her, she accepts his supremacy, assuming of her own accord the role of passively submissive wife, thus automatically adopting the traditional conjugal role pattern.[27] Always referring to him as her master, and untiring in her praise of his infinite goodness, she again and again prostrates herself before him: 'This sweet goodness overpowered all my reserves; I threw myself at his feet, and embraced his knees' (p. 193). B. and God are indivisible in her consciousness and attitude. After their wedding Pamela 'threw [herself] at his feet, blessed God, and blessed *him* for his goodness . . .' (p. 311).

Pamela can never forget the power behind her metamorphosis, the prince who transformed Cinderella into a princess. Thus she likes to wear her 'humble garb':

'. . . there will be the less reason to fear I should forget my high obligations to the kindest of gentlemen, when I can delight to show the humble degree from which his goodness has raised me' (p. 255).

On the other hand, an essential manifestation of Pamela's metamorphosis is new clothes, because dress, as Carey McIntosh points out, is 'the visible emblem of social standing'.[28] The gift of clothes is the outward sign of B.'s munificence and power. At the end of the novel B. is shown as the ideal landlord, combining the roles of judge, benevolent master, and God-like husband, with an adoring wife, weak and submissive, but strong through her husband's influence, receiving gifts and benefits from him, and in her turn bestowing benevolence and charity.

The pastoral atmosphere at the end of the novel smacks of wish fulfilment. What must have appeared as a mad dream during her worst trials has come true. At the same time, the picture of B.'s and Pamela's marriage and the roles they assume as husband and wife provide the moral exemplum which Richardson saw it as his main duty to set up for his readers.[29]

The cluster of roles and attitudes which the plot pattern reveals is even more clearly intended to serve a didactic purpose, and as we shall see, they also show up the tension between the conventional response and individual reaction at critical moments.

When Pamela's father warns her not to trust B., he has in mind a stock situation: the wicked rake of a master and the innocent country girl who is in his power. The conventional admonitory language of piousness is automatically assumed. Pamela, as we have seen, as naturally resorts to the stock response of innocence and prudishness, fostered by her strict religious upbringing. Her resistance against B.'s attempts is firmly rooted in her background. She reacts to him almost mechanically, her fainting fits being her defence mechanism. The letter form, however, emphasizes the conscious, deliberate aspect of her resistance. Once she has got over the initial shock, she uses her upbringing and consequent conviction as a means of defence against the attacker of her virtue. Pamela is always keenly aware of the principles she has been taught; they are the rock to which she clings with such tenacity.

After B.'s fall, he is naturally presented as the tempter. When sorely provoked, Pamela even calls him Lucifer. Her story soon becomes the story of the virtuous young girl in a world of sin and temptation. It is this strain in the novel Daiches has in mind when he notes its affinity to 'mediaeval saints' lives'.[30] The emphasis on trial, a cliché in pious language, suggests that the heroine is undergoing a sort of martyrdom. At the height of her suffering she writes, 'More trials, more dangers, I fear, must your poor Pamela be engaged in . . .' (p. 139).

Pamela does not simply play the role of martyr. She is ready to jeopardize her personal safety sooner than sacrifice her faith. The cliché 'trial' therefore becomes fraught with meaning for her. Repeatedly she finds herself in situations that strip her clichés and stock responses of their conventionality. She sticks faithfully to the language and roles she has been taught, but her suffering has opened her eyes to their true meaning and value. The passage in which she asserts that her soul is 'of equal importance with the soul of a princess . . .' (p. 137) abounds in well-used phrases, close to the language of orthodox Christian teaching. But we are given a strong impression that we are listening to a person whose experience has turned rather worn-out idiom into the language of personal conviction. Pamela's trials may be seen as a series of combats in which this language is tested and perfected. The way B. alternates between verbal and physical attempts on her virtue, with a certain preference for the former, favours the impression that the first half of the novel is above all concerned with the tempter's efforts to persuade the virtuous girl that the whole issue is a quibble over words. Her proverb-like, epigrammatic language, on the other hand, reveals her fundamentalist approach, and her skill is expressing what matters in simple, memorable language.

The story of Pamela's attempted seduction is intensified by being related to traditional Christian contrasts, like innocence and corruption, good and evil, above all the picture of the virtuous Christian exposed to the activities of the eternal tempter. Pamela's reflections on the queer world in which she finds herself indicate the mist of moral confusion which is one of the trials she is made to undergo. Frequently she alludes to a world in which everything appears to be upside down. After one of her debates with B. she writes: '. . . what a world we live in! for it is grown more a wonder that the men are *resisted,* than that the women *comply*' (p. 57). Pamela feels that she is at variance with a milieu in which virtue is set at naught, and where resistance to the ravisher is ridiculed as incomprehensible.

It is part of Pamela's strategy to push her values forward. She asserts her right to resist. Submitting to B.'s brutality seems a mad idea. Pamela's values are puzzling to B.'s helpers. Pamela argues that ' "... to rob a person of her virtue is worse than cutting her throat." ' Mrs. Jewkes, B.'s housekeeper on his Lincolnshire estate, finds this talk strange. ' "Are not the two sexes made for another? And is it not natural for a gentleman to love a pretty woman?" ' (p. 93). Her logic is simply horrifying to Pamela.

The moral confusion indicated here is, however, linked with a suggestion of traditional antithetic roles which may be seen as dominating sexual relationships. Man is the aggressor, woman the victim. Pamela may have been vaguely aware of this contrast in her reflection on the topsy-turvy world which surrounds her. The contrast she establishes between 'resist' and 'comply' hints at aspects of sexual relationship which are of considerable importance in the pattern of the novel.

B.'s attempts to seduce Pamela are firmly related to the rights of the individual. The would-be seducer is also a tyrant who challenges the privilege of individual freedom of choice and action. The plot in the last resort revolves round oppression–resistance–the cause of freedom, the protagonist standing for the latter, the antagonist for the former. At the same time, however, they are attributed roles which are derived from an inherited convention. Pamela, well read in romance, tends to see her attacker as the kind of giant who would abduct maidens in ancient tales of chivalry.[31] Her language reflects this kind of tale: 'oppressed innocence' (e.g. p. 83); B. is her 'unrelenting persecutor' (p. 142). Escape is constantly in her thoughts, and she longs and prays for her 'deliverance' (p. 107). As B.'s servant Pamela is 'under [his] protection' (p. 55), but his fall implies that he has failed in this chivalrous duty. Mrs. Jervis, his housekeeper, speaks the language of chivalry: she ' "never could have thought that the son of [her] dear good lady departed, could have so forfeited his honour, as to endeavour to destroy a virtue he ought to protect" ' (p. 52). These allusions to the language of romance contribute to the feeling of disintegrating values which is at the heart of Pamela's experience. She feels that B. wishes to abrogate the first clause in the code of conduct that her parents as well as her mistress had instilled into her, ' "... *be virtuous, and keep the men at a distance.* ... then comes my master: and what says he? Why, in effect it is: *Be not virtuous, Pamela!*" ' (p. 176).

The language of chivalry is traditionally exploited in religious idiom. Pamela, as usual, draws freely on it and turns it into the natural medium of her experience. Finding that all her efforts to escape from her confinement are futile, she seeks divine comfort and protection: '... God never fails to take the innocent heart into his protection, and is alone able to baffle and confound the devices of the mighty' (pp. 89–90).

28

Clearly Pamela speaks the language she has been taught, but again it is evident that the context has purged it and removed it from the habitual.

Trust in Providence is the key to Pamela's prison. Never ceasing to believe that He may and is able to do something for her, she continually sees evidence that He 'has not abandoned [her]' (p. 124). If she were to get away, she believes Providence would guide her horse (p. 137) 'and direct [her] steps to some good place of safety . . .' (p. 147). When in despair she contemplates suicide, she first determines to 'throw [herself] upon a merciful God . . .' (p. 150). She is next brought to realize that God may be testing her: 'God Almighty would not lay me under these sore afflictions, if he had not given me strength to grapple with them . . .' (p. 151). Above all, she is forced to see that 'God, who sees all the lurking vileness of [her] heart, may have permitted these sufferings on that very score . . .' (p. 151).

Providence is thus not only her knight errant who may liberate her from her prison, but also the Almighty who may uncover the secrets of the heart. Pamela is given insight into her own situation and her limitations as a human being. We are prepared for the process of humiliation and self-prostration which coincides with her metamorphosis. By trusting in God she is eventually able to trust B. and her fellow human beings.[32] Her recognition of her own worthlessness enables her to forgive even Mrs. Jewkes. Critics have felt that Richardson has allowed Pamela to go too far in self-abasement. 'There is want of taste in this humiliation; and a touch of spirit upon the occasion would not have misbecome even the all-forgiving Pamela.'[33]

But Pamela's willingness to forgive the horrible Mrs. Jewkes must be seen as a gesture which indicates the completeness of the change that is taking place in B.'s and Pamela's world. The fairytale motifs of Cinderella and persecuted maiden are subordinated to the religious motif of transgression–penitence–conversion–salvation–heavenly bliss. Mrs. Jewkes is part of the affliction God has ordained for Pamela. Once she is able to acknowledge this, forgiveness does not present itself as a problem at all. This is, however, an instance of the uneasy balance that exists at times between the didactic aim and the demands of convincing character portrayal. The forgiving Pamela is more convincing as an example of the good Christian than as an individual akin to ordinary mortals.

Pamela never doubts that B. is capable of remorse. Her friend, Mrs. Jervis, hopes that Pamela's virtuous behaviour will make him ' "ashamed of what he has done . . ." ' (p. 14). Pamela is convinced that 'God *can* touch his heart in an instant . . .' (p. 151).

Because of her steadfast refusal to surrender her virtue, Pamela miraculously finds that her 'prison is become [her] palace!' (p. 313). The magician is Providence, whose wand has touched B.'s heart.[34] The would-be rake is turned into a repentant sinner and made to confess, ' "O how heartily I despise all my former pursuits, and headstrong appetites! What joys, what true joys, flow from virtuous love . . ." ' (p. 322).' He has become the prisoner, rather than the jailor of Pamela's virtue. The role he fell from is resumed: ' "You have a generous friend, my dear girl, in me; a protector now, not a violator of your innocence . . ." ' (p. 298).

On the eve of their wedding, Pamela greets her future husband in terms of roles that are partly social, partly romantic: 'My good dear master, my kind friend, my generous benefactor; and oh! all the good words in one, my affectionate husband, that is soon to be . . .' (p. 304). The metamorphosis of the profligate rake into the virtuous husband is the overwhelming miracle that has transformed Pamela in a wordly sense and eradicated all the evil of the past. Marriage has legalized and provided a religious blessing for her strange yearning for her oppressor. Paradoxically, by resisting and enduring the trials B. inflicted upon her she offers the kind of spiritual sacrifice that eventually brings about her master's salvation.

The atmosphere of rejoicing at the end of the novel must be seen against this background. The apparently paradoxical surrender to her enemy is brought about by Providence. Pamela's heart is touched too and purged of the suspiciousness that, as we have seen, stood in the way of her future happiness. From now on the past exists merely as a source of moral example which can be studied in Pamela's letters.

After her marriage Pamela's language is continually one of rejoicing. The pattern of roles and incidents indicate a prolonged ceremony of thanksgiving, for example the occasions of public munificence, or Pamela's reiterated exclamations of gratitude. All human intercourse is completely formalized, so that one often feels that no real conversation takes place between Pamela and B. now that the days of debate are over. Her replies to his statements are general reflections or ejaculations of praise for his goodness. ' "Your goodness, Sir, . . . knows no bounds: O may my gratitude never find any!" ' (p. 417). There is a response-like quality in her exclamations, '. . . my heart is overwhelmed with his goodness' (p. 328), in striking contrast to her previous bitter laments, e.g. 'Base, wicked, treacherous gentleman . . .' (p. 73).

The didactic intention, a persistent note throughout the novel, appears to dominate completely in the latter half of the novel. Despite her stylized language and function as model wife, there is nevertheless an unmistakable flavour of genuine, personal experience. Her sincerity keeps on breaking through her ejaculations and her tendency to pose and moralize. The tendency to formulate general statements and the use of roles as moral examples are counteracted by language and situations which carry an unmistakable flavour of individual authenticity.

The individual voice keeps on breaking through; the generalizing moral observer may suddenly turn into participant. Recording how she came to love B., Pamela declares, '. . . love is not a voluntary thing . . .' (p. 220). This general reflection is followed by an account of her experience, couched in her own unmistakable style: '. . . I know not *how* it came, nor *when* it began; but it has crept, like a thief, upon me, before I knew what was the matter' (p. 220). The simile 'like a thief' is a specimen from Pamela's rich storehouse of clichés and popular idiom. But it is also peculiarly apt as a description of the way she was, without realizing it, overtaken by love. It shows how her wit is always just round the corner.

Pamela's verbal agility is shown to the full in the way she modulates 'heart', one of her favourite words, which she repeats almost to excess. Often she merely echoes common usage, as when she refers to her parents' 'honest hearts' (p. 263), or the 'black hearts' of men like B. (p. 22). The word has pride of place in the somewhat stilted language she tends to assume at solemn moments: ' ". . . dear good Sir, leave me a little to myself, and I will take myself to a severer task than your goodness will let *you* do: and present my heart before you, a worthier offering than its wayward follies will now let it seem to be" ' (p. 299).

The occasion when Pamela discovers John Arnold's treachery demonstrates, however, the way the urgency of the situation may redeem an apparently worn-out phrase like 'heart' and turn it into the natural expression of the heroine's emotional dilemma. Pamela's captivity and subsequent sudden transformation are emotional experiences that give the commonest phrase new meaning. Thus 'heart' contributes to the reverberating effect of lamentation or exultation that is a persistent quality of the language of the novel. The underlying emotional intensity makes the trite phrase strike fire. 'O my heart' and similar phrases form a basic rhythmic unit that occurs again and again when the heroine's feelings run high, often giving her style a biblical ring: 'O my exulting heart! how it throbs in my bosom . . .' (p. 223).

The road from the solemn to the colloquial is never long in Pamela's case: 'O how my heart went pit-a-pit!' (p. 222). Towards the end of the book she revisits the summer house, the scene of B.'s first attempt. She

just whipt up the steps of this once frightful place, and kneeled down, and said, 'I bless thee, O God, for my escapes, and for thy mercies! O let me always possess a grateful humble heart!' (p. 426).

In her prayer personal involvement and trite moral cliché combine to produce depth of feeling, couched in language that generations have used, in a conventional devotional attitude. Pamela affords an edifying spectacle, but we are also given a glimpse of her own situation. Her interest as a character in her own right is retained. Her despairing sigh about the 'heart of man' has been replaced by grateful trust. The passage breathes quiet conviction. The rhythm is muted, in striking contrast to the surrounding ceaseless flow of words of exultation and praise, which may at times overshadow the individual and turn her into a mere mouth-piece of sentiment.

The dilemma of the didactic writer has not been solved in *Pamela*, partly owing to the absence of correcting viewpoints. It is, however, woven into the structure of the novel. We have seen how set roles and recurrent elements in the language produce a pattern of almost auto-matic responses, related to a framework of conventional religious and moral values which a modern reader may find hard to assess. A sense of tension is achieved by placing the heroine in a number of situations in which these values are tested and filled with meaning. The merely conventional is turned into personal conviction.[35]

Open Sesame — The Persuasive Function of Pattern in George Eliot's *Silas Marner*

The open or closed door, the act of entering and leaving a room, walls and barriers of various kinds are recurrent features in *Silas Marner*. Thus the door occurs or is implied in every chapter of the novel, often in trivial contexts. The door is central in a cluster of references to everyday human affairs and activities that constitute the basis on which the action rests.

The reader is thus confronted with life as well as pattern, the latter imposing form and meaning on the former. The author's moral vision is at the heart of the pattern, giving it the kind of universal significance that Richardson sought to convey through Pamela and her letters.

Silas Marner is a mixture of legend and the kind of realism George Eliot admired in Dutch paintings.[1] F. R. Leavis remarks on 'the way in which the moral fable is realized in terms of a substantial real world.'[2] The 'moral fable' is essentially concerned with human conduct and relationship. But *Silas Marner* also contains an element of mystery which eludes the moral fable. The term 'romance' may cover this aspect, but, as R. T. Jones remarks, 'The "romance" . . . with its flavour of the marvellous, involves no thinness in the texture of reality, no relaxation of the author's grasp of the way things happen in the actual world.'[3]

The intention of this chapter is to discuss the links between 'reality', the trivial, everyday world of Raveloe, and the pattern of religious and moral behaviour and attitude which is developed in the course of the novel. Doors and barriers serve to highlight fundamental aspects of the human condition. The magic formula 'open sesame' might serve as an epigraph for the novel: harmonious relationships with other individuals, the community, and the unknown depend on the opening of doors, the pulling down of walls, in a literal as well as a figurative sense.[4] At the same time, the nearer one gets to 'them', the world beyond, the more elusive is the door, the more baffling and futile the attempt to remove the barrier between human understanding and the unfathomable.

The geographical isolation of the village of Raveloe furnishes few links with the surrounding world. The village tends to be described in

33

terms of a separate, closed world. Before the days of the railway Raveloe's position in 'the rich central plain' of England did not make for contact and openness. '. . . it was nestled in a snug well-wooded hollow, quite an hour's journey on horseback from any turnpike, where it was never reached by the vibrations of the coach-horn, or of public opinion' (p. 53).[5] The fairytale atmosphere of the novel derives in part from the fact that time does not seem to exist. The references to the number of years Silas has been in the village, or the length of time Dunstan Cass has been away suggest milestones on a road rather than the ticking of a clock.

Space is the dimension that really matters. When Silas turns up in Raveloe, it is felt that he has arrived from another world. The closed nature of 'this low, wooded region' makes it a hiding-place from the God of his old narrow community. He feels 'hidden even from the heavens by the screening trees and hedgerows' (p. 63). The village is completely isolated in a socio-economic as well as religious sense: 'Raveloe lay low among the bushy trees and rutted lanes, aloof from the currents of industrial energy and Puritan earnestness' (p. 71).

The closed nature of this community is presented in a dual light. The village is an ideal community in which neighbourliness, contentment and stability reign. Within its limits it is an open community, with the Rainbow as its natural centre, the landlord being 'bound to keep his house open to all company' (p. 106). It is the centre of good cheer over which the landlord presides with the utmost impartiality and tolerance. Significantly, it is to the Rainbow Silas goes when he has been robbed of his gold. The door is open, to him and to everybody else.

But the village is also shown to be shut off from the broadening and civilizing effect of culture, which depends on openness towards the greater world and contact with other communities. Village life and experience are recorded as aspects of primitive society: 'To the peasants of old times, the world outside their own direct experience was a region of vagueness and mystery . . .' (p. 51). The natural response to anything new and strange is fear and superstition. We are told that the narrow beliefs and customs of his community determined Silas's reaction to his epileptic fit: '. . . culture had not defined any channels for his sense of mystery . . .' (p. 57). The lack of channels, of outlets or openings characterizes the type of community we meet in *Silas Marner*. The whole narrative is suffused with an atmosphere of claustrophobia.

The initial sketch of the village indicates a closed social system:

It was an important-looking village, with a fine old church and large churchyard in the heart of it, and two or three large brick-and-stone homesteads, with well-walled orchards and ornamental weathercocks, standing close upon the road, and lifting more imposing fronts than the rectory, which peeped from the trees on the other side of the churchyard . . . (p. 53).

Squire Cass is at the top of the social hierarchy. The major families form an exclusive social circle. It was arranged that 'several neigbours should keep open house in succession' (p. 72). But the house is only open to social equals. There are frequent references to social highlights in the course of the novel, the chief of which is the New Year Party at the Red House.

The party occurs at the centre of the novel, and, like Arthur Donnithorne's birthday party in *Adam Bede*, reveals the social structure of the village as well as the villagers' attitude to their superiors. The Red House is full of guests, who all belong to the leading families of the district. The White Parlour, normally closed, is now the scene of festivity. The doors of the room underline the social pattern: 'There were two doors by which the White Parlour was entered from the hall, and they were both standing open for the sake of air; but the lower one was crowded with the servants and villagers, and only the upper doorway was left free' (p. 170).

The upper door, it is implied, is out of bounds for the lower classes. The two doors show up the chasm which divides the upper and lower classes.[6] The ordinary villagers, or the most prominent of them, are only lookers-on, not participants: 'Mr. Macey and a few other privileged villagers ... were seated on benches ... near the door ...' (p. 158). No one, however, questions the system. On the contrary, '[t]hat was as it should be – that was what everybody had been used to – and the charter of Raveloe seemed to be renewed by the ceremony' (p. 158). The parties and seasonal feasts are recurrent occasions, like the seasons of the year, highlights in a closed social system, in which every detail is 'part of the fitness of things ...' (p. 158).

The privileged few are out of touch with their social inferiors. This leads to lack of sympathy and understanding. They cannot 'enter into' the affairs of common people. The phrase is used three times during the crucial interview between Godfrey Cass and Silas towards the end of the novel when the former claims Eppie. Each time there is a suggestion of a closed world which is not open to people like Godfrey and his wife because of their social background. Godfrey 'had not had the opportunity ... of entering intimately into all that was exceptional in the weaver's experience' (p. 218). His social position accentuates his self-centredness: he 'was not prepared to enter with lively appreciation into other people's feelings ...' (p. 230). This, on the other hand, has been Silas's main concern since Eppie came to him. The social implications of the phrase are most evident in Nancy's case:

Nancy, used all her life to plenteous circumstances and the privileges of 'respectability,' could not enter into the pleasures which early nurture and habit connect with all the little aims and efforts of the poor who are born poor (p. 233).

The passage offers a final close-up of the limited and somewhat precarious nature of the upper-class world in Raveloe. In retrospect the New Year party appears on the brink of an abyss because Godfrey's wife is just at that moment on her way to the Red House to claim recognition. If death had not stopped her, she would have directed a shattering blow at the socio-moral structure of Godfrey's world. We, the readers, are allowed to travel from the world of the Red House, to the outcast world of Godfrey's wife, to Silas's cottage, another separate world, and back again to the festive gaiety of the Red House. But these three worlds are kept separate and they are largely ignorant of each other. Only Godfrey moves on a razor's edge between his own social sphere and that of his wife, a social pariah.

Godfrey's dilemma is shown clearly when Silas appears in the doorway with Eppie in his arms, at the height of the New Year party. Godfrey is struck with terror. He imagines he sees 'an apparition from that hidden life which lies, like a dark by-street, behind the goodly ornamented façade that meets the sunlight and the gaze of respectable admirers' (p. 171). The guests, who do not know what has happened, are struck by the incongruity of Silas's appearance at such a moment. We hear about their 'astonishment at this strange advent' (p. 171). The squire is angry: ' "How's this — what's this — what do you do coming in here in this way?" ' (p. 171). His hospitality, which we have previously heard 'rayed out more widely' as the evening 'deepened' (p. 152), is exposed as extremely limited.

The superficiality of approach to social inferiors is further revealed when the ladies out of curiosity are brought face to face with Silas and the baby. Even the 'good-natured Mrs. Kimble [hesitates] to take those dingy clothes into contact with her own ornamented satin boddice' (p. 172). The party is thus not open at all. It is part of the façade that surrounds the social group and isolates it from the rest of the world and natural human feelings. People like Eppie, her mother, and Silas are shut out.

In contrast, Eppie's wedding feast is arranged in 'the open yard before the Rainbow . . .' (p. 243) and appears to include the whole village, apart from the people at the Red House. The sadly closed door at the Red House (p. 242) is balanced by the account of Eppie's garden, which is 'fenced with stones on two sides, but in front there [is] an open fence, through which the flowers [shine] with answering gladness . . .' (p. 244).

The relationship between the individual and the community in which he lives is a central concern in *Silas Marner*. The open or closed door frequently illustrates the way certain characters respond to their environment. Each human being is shown to be capable of choosing between a closed and an open way of life. The characters who demonstrate the value of such a choice most clearly are Silas Marner and Godfrey Cass.

The choice itself may, however, have its origin in pure accident. It was chance that directed Eppie to Silas's door. Silas's response may have been largely instinctive, but his acts of rushing to the Red House and refusing to send Eppie to the workhouse were the results of choice between alternatives. Godfrey, on the other hand, deliberately chose to neglect his duties as a husband and father. Knoepfelmacher discusses the contrast between Silas and Godfrey in terms of the open or shut door:

Silas, by accidentally opening his door, has found the world opening to him; Godfrey, by deliberately shutting within himself the secret of his paternity, locks out even the being dearest to him, Nancy.[7]

Silas's whole life seems to be ruled by accident. The reader knows that deliberate plotting led to his misfortunes. Silas may have seen through his friend by the time he left Lantern Yard, but chance is felt to be the main director of events. The climax of the early phase in Silas's development is the scene in which his guilt is settled by means of the drawing of lots. Chance has struck him down.[8] He feels utterly lost and bewildered: 'Thought was arrested by utter bewilderment, now its old narrow pathway was closed' (p. 65). In his talk with his 'friend' before the drawing of lots, he sums up his relationship to God and man in the following words: ' "William, for nine years that we have gone in and out together, have you ever known me tell a lie? But God will clear me." ' William, however, answers: ' ". . . how do I know what you may have done in the secret chambers of your heart, to give Satan an advantage over you?" ' (p. 60).

The sunk metaphor 'gone in and out together' is an emblem of the sanctity of trust and friendship, the backbone of Silas's trust in God and man. It is also an emblem of 'natural' relationship — an order which is violated by William's act. His friend's metaphor, 'the secret chambers of your heart', is deeply ironical, as it hints at William's own closed world of deceit and betrayal. It is part of the 'message' of the novel that 'secret chambers' are incompatible with a trusting and harmonious human relationship.

In Raveloe Silas's sole refuge is his loom, at which he toils 'unremittingly' (p. 64). Utterly cut off from the community, he feels that 'there [is] nothing that call[s] out his love and fellowship toward the strangers he had come amongst . . .' (p. 65). 'call[s] out' stresses the way he almost instinctively weaves a cocoon round himself to shut out any external influence. His need for trust and love are transferred to his gold, the reward for his endless hours at the loom. Gold seems to him a perfect object for devotion because 'it [is] another element of life . . . subsisting quite aloof from the life of belief and love from which he [has] been cut off' (p. 65). He enjoys looking at the 'bright faces' of his coins. All his affection has been transferred to them. The gold 'gather[s] his power of loving together into a hard isolation like its own' (p. 92). The idea of the gold as part of a closed, but well-ordered, secure world is emphasized in a passage in which the gold and the hoarding of gold are said to have 'filled [his life] with immediate purpose which fenced him in from the wide, cheerless unknown' (p. 129). Verbs like 'cut off', 'gathered . . . together into', 'filled . . . with', 'fenced . . . in' all emphasize the passive, instinctive nature of Silas's existence. The element of deliberate action is minimal.

The cottage serves as a bulwark between Silas's gold and the 'cheerless unknown', the darkness outside, the Stone-pits. His warm, bright hearth becomes the altar at which he worships his gold:

The livelong day he sat in his loom . . . But at night came his revelry: at night he closed his shutters, and made fast his doors, and drew forth his gold (pp. 69–70).

The 'revelry' is part of his daily routine, a closed world to which no one else has access. The passage quoted suggests a ritual to keep the 'unknown' away. The magic character of such a scene is further suggested in later references to the gold. There is an obvious contrast between the scene just quoted and a later scene in which Silas mourns his lost gold:

And he sat in his robbed home through the livelong evening, not caring to close his shutters or lock his door, pressing his head between his hands and moaning, till the cold grasped him and told him that his fire was grey (pp. 140–1).

The elements in the previous scene are repeated, but the golden calf in the middle has vanished and the magic has gone: the bright fire has turned grey. References to the lost gold are accompanied by authorial comment, couched in terms that stress the claustrophobic atmosphere of Silas's existence. We are told that 'the gold . . . must be worshipped in close-locked solitude' (p. 184). It does not appear to be in Silas's power to unlock the door of his prison, and the result is complete lethargy: '. . . his soul, long stupefied in a cold, narrow prison . . .' (p. 185). The futility of his gold worship is stressed: 'The gold had kept his thoughts in an ever-repeated circle, leading to nothing beyond itself . . .' (p. 184).

After Eppie's arrival Silas's prison is gradually opened and the circle broken. His narrow world is broadened to include the whole community.[9] The door accentuates the metamorphosis Silas is undergoing.

Until the robbery Silas Marner's door had been closed to visitors. The Raveloe boys who peeped in at his window were scared away when 'opening the door', the weaver gazed at them with his queer 'protuberant' eyes (p. 52). He never invited any visitor 'to step across his door-sill' (p. 54). When the pedlar 'called at his door . . . Silas, holding the door ajar . . . said that he wanted nothing' (pp. 114–5). The door kept 'ajar' represents the absolute minimum of social contact with the outside world. His knowledge of medicinal herbs, which enabled him to help a sick woman, 'seemed to open a possibility of some fellow-ship with his neigbours . . .' (p. 65). The villagers believed that he possessed magic powers, and his cottage was 'suddenly beset by mothers who wanted him to charm away the whooping-cough, or bring back the milk, and by men who wanted stuff against the rheumatics or the knots in the hands . . .' (p. 67). Silas had seen them as intruders rather than visitors and 'drove' them away. What might have been a natural access to the Raveloe community, 'made his isolation more complete' (p. 67).

Ironically, Silas's door is unlocked on the evening Dunstan Cass robs him of his gold. On Silas's return everything at first seems normal. Anticipating his nightly revel he 'reached the door . . . opened it . . . the fire sent out a welcome increase of heat' (p. 91). After his first shock on discovering that the gold is gone, the thought of a thief makes him rush 'from his loom to the door' (p. 93). He instinctively feels the need of help from the outside and runs to the Rainbow.

The robbery does not lead to immediate contact with his neighbours, but it leads two visitors to Silas's cottage. Both pave the way for full communication.[10] The visit of the parish clerk, Mr. Macey, indicates 'of-ficial' recognition of Silas as an ordinary human being. It has become clear that he is not in league with the Evil One after all. He is urged to join the village community by buying a Sunday suit and going to church (p. 132). The other visitor, Dolly Winthrop, calls on him at Christmas and, in her way, repeats Mr. Macey's request. The way Silas receives her and her little son shows how much he has changed since he merely held the door ajar to his visitors or chased them away:

They had to knock loudly before Silas heard them; but when he did come to the door he showed no impatience, as he would once have done, at a visit that had been unasked for and unexpected. Formerly, his heart had been as a locked casket with its treasure inside; but now the casket was empty and the lock was broken. Left groping in darkness, with his prop utterly gone, Silas had inevitably a sense, though a dull and half-despairing one, that if any help came to him it must come from without; and there was a slight stirring of expectation at the sight of his fellow-men, a faint consciousness of dependence on their goodwill. He opened the door wide to admit Dolly, but without otherwise returning her greeting than by moving the arm-chair a few inches as a sign that she was to sit down in it (pp. 134–5).

The most striking feature in this passage is Silas's act of opening 'the door wide' to admit Mrs. Winthrop. Although he is underdeveloped in terms of social contact, he shows for the first time that he is capable of deliberate action. The omniscient author opens a door into Silas's mind and shows how mute and in the dark he is. But at the same time he is shown to be on the verge of closer communication with his fellow human beings. He is shown to have no words for his vague yearning for contact, but he reacts instinctively – and naturally – by opening the door wide.

It is at this moment that the process of metamorphosis starts which culminates in his adoption of Eppie. The child replaces 'the prop gone'. Her hand 'leads [Silas] forth gently towards a calm and bright land . . .' (p. 191).

The door is a central feature in the account of the process which brought Silas back to the community. Since his gold disappeared, Silas has been in 'the habit of opening his door . . . from time to time, as if he thought that his money might be somehow coming back to him . . .' (p. 166). He thinks of his golden guineas as living beings who have got lost. He feels compelled to open his door in case they should be locked out. On New Year's Eve he '[opens] his door again and again, though only to shut it immediately at seeing all distance veiled by the falling snow' (p. 167). Just as he is about to shut his door for the last time, he has one of his fits, and the door is left open. At that moment the unknown child toddles in through the door and 'right up to the warm hearth' (p. 166).

The child's appearance is as mysterious to Silas as the disappearance of his gold. At first he takes the golden-haired little girl for his lost gold. When he realizes his mistake, he still clings to the child as a kind of gold substitute. Once more he rushes out into the surrounding world to seek other people. He goes to the Red House to find the doctor. More significantly, the arrival of Eppie leads to Dolly's second visit and permanent links with normal human society.

In contrast to the closed, self-contained, barren world of the gold, Eppie's world is open and constantly expanding. She 'force[s] his thoughts onward . . .' (p. 184), out of their former narrow round. Eppie is his road 'back to nature'. We see Silas 'strolling out with uncovered head to carry Eppie beyond the Stone-pits to where the flowers grew. . .' (p. 184). Silas '[begins] to look for the once familiar herbs again . . .' (p. 185). When the memories of the past trouble him, he seeks 'refuge in Eppie's little world, that lay lightly on his enfeebled spirit' (p. 185). His new world is not a prison, but 'a soft nest' (p. 189) which he spends his time preparing for Eppie. In this limited, secluded world Eppie is protected against the harsh world outside – she '[knows] nothing of frowns and denials' (p. 189). When she is on the threshold of womanhood, we are told that '[t]he tender and peculiar love with which Silas had reared her . . . aided by the seclusion of their dwelling, had preserved her from the lowering influences of the village talk and habits . . .' (p. 205).

Silas has abandoned his previous spider-like existence. Eppie has 'created fresh and fresh links between his life and the lives from which he had hitherto shrunk ... into narrower isolation' (p. 184). He is no longer met with fear and suspicion, but 'with open smiling faces and cheerful questioning, as a person whose satisfactions and difficulties could be understood' (p. 189). 'Open' suggests that both literally and figuratively Silas's door has ceased to be closed or ajar.

As the years went by, Silas came to 'appropriate the forms of custom and belief which were the mould of Raveloe life ...' (p. 201). Eppie and Dolly Winthrop open his mind to the influences of his surroundings, and his ability to communicate with others is gradually restored. Until Eppie's arrival Silas appears to be incapable of expressing himself in words,[11] but from then on he is able to discuss the riddles of his life with Dolly. During his final interview with Godfrey Cass he is even capable of eloquent speech.

There is throughout the novel a suggestion that Silas is the victim of circumstance. He is a prisoner of the closed world in which he lives, rather than one who deliberately shuts himself off from the world. Godfrey, on the other hand, could have acted otherwise and could thus have avoided the prison of his secret marriage.

The Red House, the home of the Cass family, is a dull and cheerless place in spite of wealth and social position. The mother is dead, which means that the house lacks 'the fountain of wholesome love and fear in parlour and kitchen' (p. 72). The 'dark wainscoted parlour', with its 'half-choked fire', contains 'signs of a domestic life destitute of any hallowing charm' (p. 73).

The parlour is the scene of two interviews which illustrate Godfrey's dilemma and the lack of affection and family feeling in the Cass household. The first interview is between Godfrey and his brother Dunstan. The phrase 'The door opened' (p. 74) signals Dunstan's entrance. After a very unpleasant confrontation between the two, during which it becomes clear that he exploits his brother's secret marriage as a source of blackmail, Dunstan 'slam[s] the door behind him ...' (p. 79) and leaves Godfrey to his own dark thoughts. Imprisoned in the narrow world of his low marriage, he has a vision of two worlds which he is bound to lose if his secret is discovered. One is his own apparently secure social circle. He does not dare to tell his father about his marriage because he might then be 'turned out of house and home' (p. 74). This is the Damoclean sword that Dunstan holds over his head. Godfrey simply cannot 'imagine [any] future for himself on the other side of confession but that of 'listing for a soldier' – the most desperate step, short of suicide, in the eyes of respectable families' (p. 77). He therefore chooses rather to 'go on sitting at the feast and sipping the wine he loved, though with the sword hanging over him and terror in his heart, than rush away into the cold darkness where there was no pleasure left' (p. 77).

The other world Godfrey envisions is that of Nancy Lammeter and what he imagines life with her would be like. Life with her would be a paradise to him. The 'neatness, purity, and liberal orderliness of the Lammeter household, sunned by the smile of Nancy ...' (p. 81), appear in striking contrast to his own home 'where the hearth had no smiles ...' (p. 81), and the marriage that is 'a blight on his life' (p. 80). It seems absurd that 'this paradise ha[s] not been enough to save him from a course which shut him out of it for ever' (p. 81). When he is eventually free to marry Nancy, 'the vision of his future life seem[s] to him as a promised land ...' (p. 192). The price he has to pay for admission to this land is heavy. He does not dare to acknowledge his dead wife: 'there was one terror in his mind ... that the woman might *not* be dead' (p. 171). He fails to own his child. Authorial comment stresses the fatal development Godfrey has undergone. We are told that he used to be 'a fine open-faced good-natured young man ...' (p. 73). People have for some time suspected that 'something [was] wrong, more than common ... for Mr Godfrey didn't look half so fresh-coloured and open as he used to do' (p. 73). The full force of authorial commentary is brought to bear on Godfrey when he secretly hopes that his wife is dead: 'an evil terror – an ugly inmate [had] found a nestling-place in Godfrey's kindly disposition ...' (p. 171). 'Open', the epithet used about Godfrey's 'normal' looks, appears in ironical contrast to the 'nestling-place' of evil in his heart. We are reminded of the 'open smiling faces' (p. 189), which are Silas's reward for admitting Eppie into his home.

The second interview in the parlour is between Godfrey and his father after Dunstan's disappearance. Godfrey is forced to confess that he has given Dunstan the rent a tenant had paid him. As in the meeting between the two brothers, the dark parlour is felt to be a closed, loveless room. The shutting of the door (p. 121) indicates a hidden, secret world and lack of trust and communication. Godfrey manages to put off revealing his secret marriage. The angry squire threatens to 'turn the whole pack of [his sons] out of the house together, and marry again' (p. 123). At the same time he embarrasses Godfrey by urging him to propose to Nancy. When the young man leaves the room at the end of the interview, he resorts to 'his usual refuge ... some favourable chance which would save him from unpleasant consequences ...' (p. 126).

After Godfrey's marriage to Nancy, the Red House turns into a replica of the Lammeter household. The 'dark wainscoted parlour' is still there, but '[a]ll is purity and order in this once dreary room ...' (p. 211). Its lifelessness remains, however, because of 'the absence of children from the hearth . . .' (p. 215). Nancy is aware that Godfrey broods over this misfortune, but he does not open his mind to her.

She does not, however, know why there is not full confidence between them. Godfrey's lonely Sunday walks across his fields while Nancy reads the Bible or worries about her husband demonstrate their separateness. During such a walk Godfrey discovers that the truth about Dunstan has come to light. Godfrey opens his secret world to Nancy in the parlour. The opening of the door marks the beginning of the interview between husband and wife: 'Some one opened the door at the other end of the room . . . Nancy felt that it was her husband' (p. 221). Godfrey 'turned towards her with a pale face and a strange unanswering glance, as if he saw her indeed, but saw her as part of a scene invisible to herself' (pp. 221–2). The maid, 'already at the door' with the tea things, is turned away, and 'when the door was closed again' (p. 222), he makes a full confession of his past. The scene is once more behind closed doors, but the seclusion leads to full trust and openness between the two.

Godfrey returns to 'the oaken parlour' after his vain effort at altering the consequences of the past by claiming Eppie. Though bitterly disappointed, he is finally able to face the truth that an act once committed is past recall. The final meeting between Nancy and Godfrey in the parlour shows that Godfrey's secret world has vanished. A new shared world of complete trust and sympathy is emerging: '. . . their eyes met . . . That quiet mutual gaze of a trusting husband and wife is like the first moment of rest or refuge from a great weariness or a great danger . . .' (p. 235). Godfrey and Nancy have achieved the completeness of personal relationship which has existed all along between Eppie and Silas.

The open or closed door highlights Godfrey's and Silas's contrasting ways of responding to the lost child. Silas's door was open by accident. But his subsequent behaviour is deliberate or 'natural'. He adopts the little girl and brings her up with love and care.

Godfrey, on the other hand, fails to act according to his natural and moral duty.[12] He undergoes an ordeal of conscience while waiting outside the closed door of Silas's cottage. He feels strongly that

he ought to accept the consequences of his deeds, own the miserable wife, and fulfil the claims of the helpless child. But he had not moral courage enough to contemplate that active renunciation of Nancy as possible for him . . . (p. 174).

When the door opens and the doctor confirms that the woman is dead, he enters the cottage, but does not claim his child. His shallow question whether Marner will take the child 'to the parish' (p. 176), throws Silas's instinctive protective action towards the orphan into relief. The question implies complete renunciation, 'parish' and 'workhouse' being part of the 'cold darkness' Godfrey fears would be the consequence of confession.

The moral significance of the open or shut door – acceptance or rejection – becomes fully apparent in the scene in which Godfrey belatedly acknowledges his daughter. The chapter opens with a scene in which Silas tells Eppie how much dearer she is to him than the returned gold and how utterly lost he would be without her. A knock at the door marks the beginning of the scene in which Godfrey tells Eppie that he is her father. The onus of choice is from the beginning shown to be on Eppie. She goes 'to open the door ... and [holds] the door wide for [the Casses] to enter' (p. 227).

Silas inevitably feels that Godfrey is another external power that threatens to desolate his existence. But in contrast to the previous occasions when he was hit by disaster, he is this time confronted with a power that can be seen and approached. Class is the only gulf between them. Besides, Silas is no longer the mute, defenceless creature to whom things simply happen. Encouraged by Eppie's firm refusal of the Casses' offer to adopt her – ' "I can't leave my father ... I couldn't give up the folks I've been used to" ' (p. 230)[13] – Silas finds strength to challenge Godfrey's authority. He feels 'the spirit of resistance in him set free ...' (p. 230) and answers Godfrey with unusual directness and eloquence:

'... why didn't you say so sixteen year ago, and claim her before I'd come to love her, i'stead o' coming to take her from me now, when you might as well take the heart out o' my body? God gave her to me because you turned your back upon her, and He looks upon her as mine: you've no right to her! *When a man turns a blessing from his door, it falls to them as take it in*' (p. 231). (My italics).

Silas uses the door in a moral proverb which brings out the finality of Godfrey's choice when he failed to acknowledge his child. Fate may have chosen the door, but once the child had turned up, it challenged deliberate action. *Adam Bede* demonstrates the impossibility of escaping the consequences of any act, whether the act is avoidable or not. In *Silas Marner* the emphasis is on the far-reaching and irrevocable consequences of deliberate action. Repentance and an earnest wish to make amends cannot alter past action, or, as Silas puts it, 'repentance doesn't alter what's been going on for sixteen year' (p. 231).

In the last resort the act of choice falls on Eppie. In contrast to her father, she possesses no hidden worlds to trouble her conscience. She unhesitatingly chooses Silas and the 'little home where he'd sit in the corner ...' (p. 234). She sticks to the 'working-man' she has promised to marry, despite the fact that Godfrey 'opens his home' to her and offers her all the benefits of his social status (p. 234). When the Casses are back in the Red House, it is Silas's words 'about a man's turning away a blessing from his door . . .' (p. 236) that stick in Godfrey's mind. He now realizes the full force of the truth that an act is irrevocable and that no compensation can remove its consequences.

The scene in which Eppie rejects her father marks the end of Silas's long period of confrontation with a puzzling existence. Everything that had happened to him previously seemed to emerge from a mysterious, closed world to which he and his neighbours had no access. The disappearance of his gold remained for sixteen years a riddle that no detective work could unravel. On Eppie's sudden appearance Silas sums up his situation in the following words: ' ". . . the door was open. The money's gone I don't know where, and this is come from I don't know where" ' (p. 179).

The strange and mysterious is an element that runs right through the novel. Recurrent words like 'strange', 'mysterious', 'mystery', 'riddle' converge on the central meaning of something inexplicable, beyond the scope of human understanding. The mysterious belongs to a world which is closed to Silas and his neighbours. They all appear from time to time to be groping in the dark for a door into this realm. Dolly has a very simply theory about the arrival of the child: ' ". . . there's Them as took care of it, and brought it to your door . . ." ' (p. 179).

The villagers assembled in the Rainbow illustrate two basic approaches to the mysterious. The sceptics are convinced that the disappearance of Silas's money can be rationally explained. If the facts were known, the mystery would disappear. The 'believers' attribute Silas's misfortunes to 'powers' belonging to the supernatural sphere and therefore beyond reach. Both the gold and the child fit into a system of mysterious interference from a supernatural world.

There are, however, two different views of this world among the 'believers'. For Mr. Macey and his followers supernatural interference is a matter of dogma. They feel that their prestige and personal honour are at stake when the sceptics challenge them on supernatural subjects like the existence of ghosts.

Dolly Winthrop, on the other hand, humbly accepts the existence of a mysterious world she feels surrounds her, while at the same time trying to penetrate it with her intellect. She is convinced of the existence of 'Them' above, and seeks to find an entrance to the world of Providence. Her approach is that of common sense and wisdom, collected during years of good works. She responds with her heart as well as with her mind. Her main channel of contact is her tact and sympathy. It puzzles Silas that he cannot explain the disappearance of his gold or the arrival of the child. During her talk with Silas on this subject Dolly reveals her belief in mysterious contact with the invisible world of 'Them', as well as her intellectual bent:

'... it's like the night and the morning, and the sleeping and the walking, and the rain and the harvest – one goes and the other comes, and we know nothing how nor where. We may strive and scrat and fend, but it's little we can do arter all – the big things come and go wi' no striving o' our'n ... I think you're in the right on it to keep the little un, Master Marner, seeing as it's been sent to you ...' (pp. 179–180).

Dolly sees the world beyond sense perception in terms of the world she knows. The abstract and intangible are felt to be a concrete presence. This feeling lends force to her idea that Eppie has been sent to Marner.

Apart from the child, Dolly is the main instrument in leading Silas away from his narrow isolation. When he first holds the child on his knee, he trembles 'with an emotion mysterious to himself, at something unknown dawning on his life' (p. 180). He feels vaguely that he has been brought up against a world which Dolly might help him to understand. She persuades him to go to church and have Eppie christened. He has no 'distinct idea' about these matters, 'except that Dolly had said it was for the good of the child ...' (pp. 183–4).

Dolly helps him to accept what has happened in the past, however unjust and inexplicable it may have appeared to be. Silas's misfortunes are as puzzling to her as to him, but her reason and feeling tell her that there must be a solution to his mystery, thought it may be beyond human reach: ' "... there's trouble i' this world, and there's things as we can niver make out the rights on" ' (p. 204). She can offer Silas sympathy and a simple moral guideline. The door she holds open for him is her conviction that as

'Them above has got a deal tenderer heart [than human beings] all as we've got to do is to trusten ... to do the right thing as fur as we know, and to trusten ... And if you could but ha' gone on trustening, Master Marner, you wouldn't ha' run away from your fellow creatures and been so lone' (pp. 204–5).

Guided by Dolly, Silas acknowledges that ' "[t]here's good i' this world ... That drawing o' the lots is dark; but the child was sent to me: there's dealings with us – there's dealings" ' (p. 205). Silas has recovered his belief in divine interference and learnt to accept it. After his vain effort to get to the bottom of the Lantern Yard mystery, he reconciles himself to the fact that certain matters will forever remain mysterious. At the end of the novel he is fully convinced of the truth of Dolly's wisdom:

'Since ... the child was sent to me and I've come to love her as myself, I've had light enough to trusten by; and now she says she'll never leave me, I think I shall trusten till I die' (p. 241).

The mysterious is still part of an invisible, closed world. But Silas has become able to accept this circumstance and at the same time see that there is a benevolent power which *sends* blessings and provides *light* 'enough to trusten by', i.e. sufficient happiness and understanding or knowledge to play one's part in the community.

The open door and light-symbolism tend to be linked in *Silas Marner*, as on the occasions when Dunstan steals the gold and Eppie finds her way to Silas's hearth. In the passage just quoted it is related to moral insight or guidance, and the problem of understanding matters that pertain to be the hidden, spiritual world. When Dolly puzzles over Silas's mysterious past, the truth she feels is hidden in it suddenly comes to her 'as clear as daylight' (p. 203). There are references throughout the novel to the 'inner light' of religious communities like the Methodists. The idea of revealed insight may be expressed in terms of entering an open doorway, as when Dolly says ' "it come to me all clear . . ." ' (p. 203), or ' "it all come pouring in . . ." ' (p. 204).

Barbara Hardy comments on the frequency with which the character with a limited or undeveloped understanding occurs in Georg Eliot's early fiction.[14] The omniscient point of view is used to interpret and communicate what is in the minds of characters who cannot think or express themselves clearly. Silas Marner's development from a completely apathetic creature to one who communicates freely with his fellow human beings is accentuated by the extensive use of the omniscient approach in the first half of the novel. After the arrival of Eppie there is a gradual transfer of focus from author to character.

Throughout the novel the author tends to provide an opening into the closed worlds of primitive or limited minds. The author may create the impression of a vacuum, of an underdeveloped reasoning faculty. She may also provide close-ups of a mind at work on some problem that is beyond its capacity. Often we are shown a character grappling with the problem of expressing ideas that are only vaguely understood. Dolly is particularly sensitive to the nuances of meaning and the power and the value of words. On the one hand she is painfully aware that she has 'a deal [inside her] as'll niver come out . . .' (p. 203), as if her mind is a kind of prison. It is in keeping with her general approach to the hidden that she endeavours to find words for the mysterious and understand 'the meaning o' what [she] hears at church . . .' (p. 202). On the other hand, Dolly's rational approach to language is balanced by her primitive belief in 'good' words: she prints letters on her cakes without understanding their meaning. She feels they are part of a separate existence and may serve as a magic door to a hidden world.

Silas combines the two attitudes. He has to learn the language of ordinary society and to apply his rational gift to the overwhelming mystery he has had to live with so long. But he also learns to appreciate the emotional value of communion with the hidden spiritual world in which 'good' words may have a ritual function.

A striking feature in the element of mystery as a closed and separate system is the suggestion of a labyrinth which so often creeps round its edges. The topography and climate of Raveloe at first sight appear peaceful, calm, and harmonious. But on closer inspection the setting has a maze-like pattern. This is clear on a number of occasions which are of crucial importance in the story.

The first occasion is when Dunstan gropes his way through darkness, mist, and rain to Silas's cottage and steals the gold. Godfrey's whip and Silas's light guide him out of the labyrinth which the well-known lane has become. When he turns his back on the light and cannot use the whip, 'he [steps] forward into the darkness' (p. 90), i.e. death.

The snow-filled lanes are only a nuisance to the guests at the Casses' New Year party. But they are a mortal danger to Godfrey's wife. She loses her way, and is, anyway, lost in the labyrinth of opium, and dies a few steps from Silas's door. It is as if the labyrinth in her case too leads to Silas, and inevitable destruction. The child, whose senses are not dulled by opium, escapes from the labyrinth because of Silas's open door and bright hearth.

When Godfrey hears of the dead woman outside Silas's cottage, he rushes into the snow-covered lane. He, however, only gets his feet wet. Figuratively, he is, nevertheless, shut up in a maze of sin and guilt, in which he remains a prisoner for sixteen years. His restless pacing to and fro in the snow outside Marner's door while he is waiting for confirmation that his wife is dead, is emblematic of his whole existence during the time he kept his first marriage secret.

The figure of the maze is particularly important in Silas's case. The circle or closed world with which he surrounds himself after his flight from Lantern Yard is a labyrinth in which there appears to be no opening. His tiny circle represents the 'state of nullity and unreality' in which Barbara Hardy feels that Silas's tragedy lies.[15] The circle encloses a vacuum, complete emptiness, which is filled by the gold. The gold, on the other hand, as we have heard previously, keeps 'his thoughts in an ever-repeated circle ...' (p. 184). Like the captives in the labyrinth, he soon loses his bearings.

On the other hand, his labyrinth-like existence makes him forget the bewilderment he experienced when the 'old narrow pathway [of his old creed] was closed' (p. 65). One labyrinth is substituted for another. Characteristically, when he loses his gold, bewilderment returns: his 'thoughts could no longer move in their old round' (p. 129). Habit and routine are mazes he follows blindly, and oddly enough he only feels pent-up and lost when the essential elements in his routine have gone, i.e. when the maze has disappeared.

Eppie brings Silas out of the maze of dreariness and routine. His ability to communicate with his neighbours also enables him to find words for his sense of being the prisoner of mysterious 'powers'. After having talked to Dolly about the puzzling disappearance of his gold and the equally puzzling arrival of the child, he adds, ' "I'm partly mazed" ' (p. 176). Silas is of course merely using a common expression, but the whole context makes the underlying sense of being lost in a labyrinth approach the surface and subtly deepens the meaning of Marner's everyday phrase.[16] Silas makes his own diagnosis, and by doing so, he starts his process of recovery. Eppie's open garden fence at the end of the story is as far removed from the labyrinth as possible. It suggests a way of life that is both open and protected; the happy family circle is not shut off from the world.

The door is part of the reality of the village of Raveloe. It indicates the human need for social organization and communication. The novel reflects man's instinct for order and security. The recurrence of 'door' and related words forms a pattern which suggests that the novel presents an ordered, coherent version of a reality which is by comparison formless and chaotic. At the same time, the door represents the aspects of reality which man's social instinct has created. Chaos is part of the darkness that is so much feared in the novel.

Fable and myth may be seen as attempts to impose order and meaning on the darkness that surrounds man. The door as it is used in *Silas Marner* pertains to both. The pattern it forms is part of a universal pattern which concerns the moral code that governs man's existence in this world and his relationship to the unknown which surrounds it. The door stands for man's ability to perceive links between himself and the universe, in both a moral and a mystical sense. It is also evidence of the existence of such a universe.

Fear is a predominant emotion in *Silas Marner,* but it never permanently defeats man's capacity for joy. The door frequently suggests the power of the intuitive instinct; the heart is often a surer guide than the head. A number of 'door passages', often of the most trivial kind, stress the need for and ability to establish emotional contact with one's surroundings, human and superhuman, however inexplicable they may be.

In *Silas Marner* the legendary and everyday are closely linked. The emphasis on open and closed doors, walls and barriers brings out this dual effect of the novel. The author clearly has a lesson she wishes to teach her readers, but the didactic impulse has been channelled into the texture of the novel.

CHAPTER III

Thomas Hardy, *The Mayor of Casterbridge*
The Persuasive Function of Character

Pamela and *Silas Marner* demonstrate two approaches to the moral writer's problem of reconciling the requirements of the novel form with his urge to teach. The novelist of ideas is faced with a similar problem: How can he present his thoughts in such a form that they seem an integral part of the novel? His problem is not least one of communication: how to persuade his readers to accept his ideas, at least for the duration of their reading experience. Hardy seems to have been faced with the dilemma of reconciling his dogmatic need for inarticulate characters, who illustrate the view that man is a tiny creature that blindly collides with an inscrutable fate, with his need for a character who can perceive and articulate this bleak vision. The main characters in *The Mayor of Casterbridge* are a case in point.

Henchard is usually, and rightly, considered the central character in *The Mayor of Casterbridge*. The novel is after all named after him. George Wing feels that the 'former hay-trusser dwarfs the rest of the characters.'[1] Irving Howe shows that 'Hardy's design requires that, to sharpen the contrast between looming protagonist and the secondary figures, Henchard be scaled as somewhat larger than life . . .'[2]

His greatness is, however, of a kind that he himself cannot express. He is, like some of George Eliot's early characters – for example Tulliver (*The Mill on the Floss*) or Adam Bede, strangely inarticulate. He is a volcano, erupting elemental energy, but he is usually only vaguely aware of the range and significance of his actions. Henchard has the strength of a bull, but intellectually he appears to be rather dim. He is the helpless victim of circumstances rather than one who combines physical force and impulsive energy with brilliant intellect in his efforts to tame his hostile surroundings. Henchard's metamorphosis from poor hay-trusser to rich corn-merchant and powerful mayor belongs to the world of legend.[3] There are few indications that he has the intellectual capacity for such a drastic change of circumstances.

This is of course hardly fair to Henchard. Hardy's whole point is that the Mayor, physically and temperamentally, is well equipped for the role of protagonist. With his animal strength, his uncontrollable energy, and certain quirks of temperament, he demonstrates Hardy's view that man is the sport of circumstance and fate. Seen against a background of a hostile and indifferent universe, man may put up a gallant struggle – against an adversary he does not know, but the outcome, defeat, is inevitable. The reader is shown the discrepancy between protagonist and antagonist. The dogged fight against overwhelming odds provides a novel like *The Mayor of Casterbridge* with an heroic dimension.

Seen from a sufficient distance and placed in an appropriate cosmic context, any hero will seem pathetic and fragile. Yet we are not allowed to lose our sense of proportion in a world which is after all anthropocentric. Man and his world may be a whim, but once this whim has materialized, we are imprisoned by it, unable to penetrate far beyond it. The narrator in Hardy's novel may adopt a god-like position, but he cannot cut the links with the human world and lose himself in the void of outer space.

In *The Mayor of Casterbridge* the narrator combines the vast view of the gods which reduces the world of men to an ant-heap, and the approach of the scientist who with his microscope and camera detects and magnifies this tiny world.[4] This cold, objective approach is qualified by the note of irony in the god-like narrator's voice. J. Hillis Miller sees this voice

as a compound of irony, cold detachment, musing reminiscent bitterness, an odd kind of sympathy which might be called 'pity at a distance,' and, mixed with these, a curious joy, a grim satisfaction that things have, as was foreseen, come out for the worst in this worst of all possible worlds.[5]

'Pity at a distance' and 'grim satisfaction' are countered by the natural human unwillingness to face the worst. Characters, readers, even author shrink from the abyss of nihilism and absence of all hope. The refusal to give in, however absurd, is part of the human appeal of the novel. Another 'humanizing' feature in a novel like *The Mayor of Casterbridge* is the picture we are given of 'normal' society. The daily rhythm of the community serves as a backcloth to the protagonist's heroic, but hopeless ordeal. Ordinary life goes on, despite the suffering of the people in the foreground. This is part of the cruelty of circumstance, the general indifference to the fate of the individual. But on reading the novel, we tend, perhaps because we share the human predicament, to interpret certain elements as signs of hope: the changing seasons, for example, or references to the rhythm of the daily life of the community, at work or on festive occasions.

The most important 'humanizing' factor in *The Mayor of Casterbridge* is, however, Henchard's step-daughter, Elizabeth-Jane. Although she is deliberately toned down, her 'role is an extraordinarily interesting one . . .'[6], not least from a technical viewpoint. She is the only character in the novel who consistently adopts the role of spectator. One suspects that she shares the narrator's detached approach to the community to which she belongs.[7] But, as we shall see, she also shares the sum of human experience which is portrayed in the novel. Unlike the narrator, she is also victim and participant. Like the other characters, she is at times held at arm's length and scrutinized by him. Is Elizabeth-Jane a means of bridging the gap between the lofty, somewhat inhuman heights of the narrator and the puny human world he is so keen on exposing?

Elizabeth-Jane, or her half-sister, first appears to the reader as a victim. During the auction scene in Chapter I, in which Henchard sells his wife, the little girl on her mother's lap is utterly unconscious of what is happening, although her whole future is at stake. The mother–child image calls up in the reader instincts like protection, innocence, the sanctity of the family. The woman and her daughter seem to stand for suffering humanity. Henchard, on the other hand, is felt to violate the basic laws of human society.

Douglas Brown stresses the role that the idea of property plays in the novel. Even human relationship is evaluated in commercial terms. Susan Henchard, in agreeing to be sold, 'reflects her credence in purchase power and in society's complicity in that power.'[8] Henchard is the hero of a novel 'about transition'.[9] But although economic and social laws are shown to be at work from the beginning, we are primarily made to respond in terms of 'natural' family feeling. Hardy does not intend us to condemn Henchard outright, but wishes us to see the auction episode in the perspective of the whole novel.

Perhaps the most serious of the sins that later dog him so mercilessly is his failure as husband and father in the initial scene. It is at the core of the curse he does not manage to remove from his life, despite his later efforts to make amends. The fatal action is, of course, also indicative of a flaw in his character: his tendency to make decisions on the spur of the moment; he is entirely guided by impulse. Despite his ability to keep a vow for twenty-one years, there is a streak of irresponsibility in his character, of ruthless egocentricity, which his 'good' moments cannot compensate or guard against.

The role of victim implies passivity, that a person is more acted against than acting. The sleeping child in the auction scene is the image of powerlessness and ignorance. The two elements persist in the image of the victim that Elizabeth-Jane represents in the novel. She illustrates one of the major ways in which fate manifests itself in the world of Hardy's novels – that of irony. We, the readers, are made aware of the discrepancy between appearance and reality. Although Susan Henchard is re-united with her husband, the truth of their past relationship is withheld from Elizabeth-Jane. Ignorant of the disgraceful past, she thinks of herself all the time as Henchard's step-daughter, a mere appendage. This no doubt influences her whole behaviour and attitude to the Mayor. She comes to regard him as her benefactor, with no obligations towards her, except that she is the daughter of his wife. Fate makes Henchard reveal what he thinks is the truth about his relationship to Elizabeth-Jane moments before his dead wife's letter reveals that the daughter he had sold is dead. Henchard cannot bring himself to tell the girl that she is not his daughter after all. But neither is he able to behave as a father towards her.

The result is that Elisabeth-Jane's role as suffering victim is reinforced. She sees something has gone wrong, but is in the dark about the cause. She is, in other words, the prototype of mankind suffering under the yoke of an impenetrable fate.

H. C. Duffin feels that the girl 'fails miserably'[10] when during her wedding she refuses to forgive Henchard for having kept her from her real father. But the very fact that Elizabeth-Jane here departs from her attitude of passive acquiescence to fate is after all natural. For one thing, she has all along been a staunch supporter of respectability.[11] This is clear on the occasion when her mother goes to see the furmity woman about Henchard (p. 26).[12] Her sense of what is respectable makes her leave Lucetta when she marries Farfrae and fails to marry Henchard, which Elizabeth-Jane claims is her duty (pp. 215–17). Henchard's deception is another breach of propriety. But worse than this is that once again he has broken sacred family ties. By keeping her in the dark about her real father so long, and by telling her father she is dead, he has, in her view, deliberately wronged them. Granted, her version of the truth is warped. It is one of the ironies of the novel that the final truth is inaccessible, partly because Henchard is too proud to defend himself, partly because trust has broken down between them, and his words would therefore not have been believed.

Elizabeth-Jane's final speech to Henchard shows that she is still a victim, speaking and acting from ignorance:

'I could have loved you always – I would have, gladly ... But how can I when I know you have deceived me so – so bitterly deceived me! You persuaded me that my father was not my father – allowed me to live on in ignorance of the truth for years; and then when he, my warm-hearted real father, came to find me, cruelly sent him away with a wicked invention of my death, which nearly broke his heart. O how can I love as I once did a man who has served us like this!' (p. 326).

It is as if the emotions and bewilderment bottled up over the years finally find release in the language of natural affection. The reference to the warm-hearted Newson throws her sufferings in Henchard's cold and hostile home into relief. On the other hand, she responds conventionally as well, as the dutiful daughter. We are reminded of the fairly easy transference of feelings from Newson to Henchard when the latter claims he is her father (pp. 123 and 130). She now reacts so violently because by keeping her in the dark, her stepfather has behaved monstrously. He has in a way kidnapped her and deprived her of her natural rights. When she transferred her affections to Henchard, she behaved naturally, both because she cared for him – there is evidence of her affection in her denouncement of him now – and because as a woman and daughter it is her natural duty to submit. It is part of her role as victim to submit to a false father – without her knowledge.

However, the reader probably instinctively feels that Elizabeth-Jane's harsh words to her stepfather are an act of rejection, unfair despite the past, and cruel. This is partly because of Henchard's situation: he is crushed by fate, and only a shadow of his old self. We, the readers, automatically feel pity for him. He stands there as a victim, not as the author of his own misery. In addition, the narrator has provided us with all the facts and a full knowledge of Henchard's character and the change he has undergone. The narrator's commentary after Elizabeth-Jane's denunciation supplements her version of the truth. The perspective she lacks is provided. Henchard is one who has diced for happiness in one 'last desperate throw.' It is not that he is too proud to plead his cause, it is 'that he [does] not sufficiently value himself to lessen his sufferings by strenuous appeal or elaborate argument' (p. 326). In his humility he commands our respect more than he did at the height of his glory.

All the characters in *The Mayor of Casterbridge* are victims in that things happen to them which they have no means of averting. They fall into three categories as regards the way they respond to the chain of events that keeps them prisoners: those who grimly fight back or try to master circumstances – by brute force (Henchard), or skill (Farfrae); those who submit and endure fate with stoic calm (Elizabeth-Jane); and those any crisis drives to hysteria (Lucetta).

Her long period of suffering and neglect reveals Elizabeth-Jane's strength of endurance. She does not do anything to change her circumstances beyond moving from her father's house when, significantly, accident offers her an opportunity. Ironically, one of her few deliberate actions lands her deeper into the quagmire of fate. Her decision to go and stay at High Place Hall leads Farfrae, just when the road seems open for Elizabeth-Jane, straight to Lucetta. The former never discovers how nearly she missed 'happiness'. Henchard may treat his stepdaughter as a pawn in his deadly struggle with Farfrae – alternately forbidding and inviting the Scotsman to court her – and Farfrae may notice her or not depending on his mood or state of business. The indifference these men show accentuates her role as a victim, the submissive woman whom custom and temperament have barred from being the custodian of her own future. A 'dumb, deep-feeling, great-eyed creature' (p. 134), she is the prototype of the victim in the novel. Her unrequited love for Farfrae confirms this impression.

Love, David Cecil tells us, is a favourite disguise for fate in Hardy's fiction.[13] This is clear from beginning to end in *The Mayor of Casterbridge*, from the picture of married boredom to that of frustrated love for the girl who turns out not to be the daughter, but is nevertheless the dream of a daughter. Between these two 'pictures' there are a number of others, all related to the various phases of the changing relationships between Henchard, Lucetta, Farfrae and Elizabeth-Jane.

'Picture' seems a suitable word to describe the pattern of relationships that is woven between the central characters. So much of the effect is pictorial, one of contrasts, of a constant play of light and shadow. This impression is based on the fluctuations which these relationships undergo, so closely related to the business and social careers of the men. But the contrasts are above all related to temperament and milieu.

Elizabeth-Jane is particularly important for the pictorial effect of the novel. She combines her role as victim, 'the receiving spirit',[14] with that of the foil, the character who sets off the other central characters. Duffin draws attention to the pictorial effect of this type of character: 'She is drawn in such pale tones that there is some danger of the exquisite beauty of the picture being lost under the fierce colouring of the two male portraits.'[15] George Wing feels that all the other characters have been 'muted' to set off Henchard, but he singles out Elizabeth-Jane as a foil of a particular kind: '. . . partly because she was an emotional foil for Henchard, Elizabeth-Jane moves occasionally into spheres of meek heroism.'[16] Henchard reacts violently, with all his physical force and emotional ferocity, to the challenge of a crisis. His heroism is that of a man who cannot submit patiently, but will fight any adversary with dauntless courage. The elemental strength with which he opposes any obstacle in his way is finely brought out the evening he reveals to Elizabeth-Jane that he is her father:

His mind began vibrating between the wish to reveal himself to her and the policy of leaving well alone, till he could no longer sit still. . . He could no longer restrain his impulse. 'What did your mother tell you about me – my history?' (p. 124).

Then follows his abrupt revelation of what has been hidden so long. He does not give her any time to arrange her thoughts, although he says he will give her time to think. His words and his behaviour are in conflict: ' "I don't want you to come to me all of a sudden," said Henchard in jerks, and moving like a great tree in a wind' (p. 125). The tree in the wind is a perfect image of Henchard's type of heroism. It can never yield, but it can be destroyed.

Elizabeth-Jane's type of heroism is shown up in the interview too.

Henchard is moved by long pent-up passion. She is utterly unprepared, except that she is used to the ups and downs of fate. But the emotional impact of her stepfather's revelation effects her in a diametrically opposite way to Henchard's turbulent response to the crisis. While his feelings force him to walk up and down the room, '[t]he back of Elizabeth's head [remains] still, and her shoulders [do] not denote even the movements of breathing' (p. 124). In a closeup we are shown the girl after Henchard has left the room. She is meditating on her changed circumstances, trying to 'adjust her filial sense to the new centre of gravity' (p. 126). She is silently mourning 'the genial sailor Richard Newson, to whom she [seems] doing a wrong' (p. 126). Henchard's turbulence is put into relief. Her quiet submission when she has thought the matter over has a similar effect.

Elizabeth-Jane tends to behave like this at a moment of crisis. She does not, like Henchard, react impulsively, but uses her intellect and reflective power. On another occasion we are told that '[w]hen she walked abroad she seemed to be occupied with an inner chamber of ideas...' (p. 98). She possesses an inner reserve which enables her to bear her loneliness during Henchard's neglect. 'Susan Henchard's daughter bore up against the frosty ache of the treatment, as she had borne up under worse things...' (p. 175). The occasion is a meeting between Farfrae and Lucetta. When the latter tells her that the two have married, Elizabeth-Jane's one request is, ' "Let me think of it alone" ... corking up the turmoil of her feeling with grand control' (p. 217). Henchard, too, may at critical moments give the impression of suppressed feeling, but in his case a volcanic eruption seems imminent. His 'grand control' certainly does not entail outward calm. His fortitude is 'Titanic',[17] Elizabeth-Jane's is that of Ruth 'amid the alien corn...'

Elizabeth-Jane's role as a foil is particularly striking in her friendship with Lucetta. The two of them are akin, most clearly in their relationship to Farfrae, to the Romantic contrasting pair of women – the docile, domestic, fair-haired type, and the passionate, exotic, dark-haired one. The former is not at first noticed by the man she falls in love with. He is inevitably drawn to the latter, with whom he has a turbulent, but transient affair. Bruised and disillusioned he is of course in the end guided to the safe haven of the Gretchen type of woman.

Apart from the colour of their hair Lucetta and Elizabeth-Jane are reminiscent of these two types. Lucetta is flashy and hysterically keen on cathing her man, although she is but a shadow of the Romantic demonic, passionate woman. She has nevertheless considerable charm and instantaneous sex appeal, as is shown during the first meeting between her and Farfrae (pp. 158 ff.). It soon becomes evident that she is rather shallow, a mere plaything. The relationship between her and Farfrae does not appear to be taken quite seriously:

As on the Sunday, so on the week-days, Farfrae and Lucetta might have been seen flitting about the town like two butterflies – or rather like a bee and a butterfly in league for life (p. 235).

It is as if life is too serious an affair for such a relationship to survive – at least the butterfly seems too tender to last long, while the bee has a more tenacious hold on life. The insect images reflect Hardy's tendency to reduce man to the infinitesimal. Lucetta's premature death as a consequence of the shock of the skimmity ride is foreshadowed. Her butterfly existence is crushed out by harsh reality.

G. G. Urwin refers to the view that Elizabeth-Jane 'is to some extent a re-casting of Amelia Sedley in *Vanity Fair* and all that host of pathetic young ladies for whom all eventually turned out well' – a view he regards as 'untrue'.[18] There is nevertheless a typological link. Seen in the company of Lucetta, she belongs to the family of pale heroines. In her own eyes she is plain. As we have seen, neither Henchard nor Farfrae are struck by her, as they are by Lucetta or by each other. Elizabeth-Jane's insistence on respectability and propriety of behaviour gives her a touch of the Victorian prude. In contrast to Lucetta, her sexual instincts are kept under strict control. Unlike Lucetta, Elizabeth-Jane does nothing to encourage Farfrae from her first meeting with him during their talk after their first and only dance, until their wedding long afterwards. Her complete passivity is shown up when Farfrae seems on the verge of 'popping the question':

'I wish I was richer, Miss Newson; and your stepfather had not been offended; I would ask you something in a short time – yes, I would ask you tonight. But that's not for me!'

What he would have asked her he did not say, and instead of encouraging him she remained incompetently silent (p. 112).

The 'good moment' passes and does not occur again. Elizabeth-Jane bears her frustrated love for Farfrae with the same fortitude she displays in every crisis. Lucetta's hysteria is balanced by her friend's imperturbable calm: '. . . she viewed with an approach to equanimity the now cancelled days when Donald had been her undeclared lover . . .' (p. 180).

Married to Farfrae at last, Elizabeth-Jane is shown in a domestic rather than a passionate context. There is nothing of the butterfly about her activities as a wife. After a month she has 'grown accustomed to the novelty of her situation . . .' (p. 327). At the end of the novel we see her 'in a latitude of calm weather . . . the lively and sparkling emotions of her early married life cohered into an equable serenity . . .' (p. 333). The marriage between Farfrae and Elizabeth-Jane may serve as a foil to his more spectacular union with Lucetta, and can be seen as a Richardsonian example of the ideal marriage. It is indeed a foil that proves to be of an enduring kind, because the relationship between the two is not wholly dependent on the passion of love.

Elizabeth-Jane's role as foil to Lucetta is brought out by the two girls' way of dressing. Clothes imagery is as important in *The Mayor of Casterbridge* as in *Pamela*. It serves a similar didactic-emblematic purpose to that of Henchard's career from haytrusser to Mayor and back to labourer and haytrusser. Each stage is accompanied by a change of clothes. Social status is indicated, but we are also given hints of the wearer's personality and moral stature.

On her first appearance the plainness of Elizabeth-Jane's dress is emphasized. This underlines her poverty as well as her unspectacular looks. The social metamorphosis she undergoes as a result of her mother's 'marriage' to Henchard is reflected in her way of dressing. Her oldfashioned, though respectable outfit (p. 72) is gradually replaced by the apparel that makes her more interesting in the eyes of Casterbridge. She is, however, reticent:

She formed curious resolves on checking gay fancies in the matter of clothes, because it was inconsistent with her past life to blossom gaudily the moment she had become possessed of money (p. 98).

Her behaviour sets her up as an example: her sudden riches do not make her vain or too full of her own importance. Characteristically, when her stepfather cold-shoulders her, she automatically becomes more modest in terms of clothes and general behaviour. She confines herself to her lonely room, and her only walks seem to be to the churchyard. Before setting out into the drizzle, she

went to the boot-room where her pattens had hung ever since her apotheosis; took them down, had their mildewed leathers blacked, and put them on as she had done in old times (p. 144).

It is as if she consummates the rejection Henchard has effected in his mind and behaviour, and returns, at least for the moment, to her past humble station.

By now she has, however, met Lucetta. On a previous visit she had seen, but did not speak to a strange woman sitting by her mother's grave. She had felt instinctively drawn to her, and it was her dress she first noticed:

The personage was in mourning like herself, was about her age and size, and might have been her wraith or double, but for the fact that it was a lady much more beautifully dressed than she. Indeed, comparatively indifferent as Elizabeth-Jane was to dress, unless for some temporary whim or purpose, her eyes were arrested by the artistic perfection of the lady's appearance. ... It was a revelation to Elizabeth that human beings could reach this stage of external development ... She felt all the freshness and grace to be stolen from herself on the instant by the neighbourhood of such a stranger (pp. 135-6).

The two women are alike and absolute contrasts at the same time. Elizabeth-Jane is evidently fascinated by the strange lady's exterior, but totally ignorant of her real character. There is a hint that she is about to be deluded by appearance. Such a possibility is also suggested in the following comment by the narrator, to the effect that Elizabeth's sense of inferiority 'was in face of the fact that Elizabeth could now have been writ handsome, while the young lady was simply pretty' (p. 136). It soon becomes clear, however, that it is not only Elizabeth-Jane who is captivated by the lady's beauty and elegance. Lucetta soon, as we have seen, blinds Farfrae to the unostentatious excellence of Henchard's stepdaughter.

We must bear in mind Elizabeth-Jane's circumstances when she meets Lucetta. She is starved of affection and company, utterly neglected by Henchard, and has no friends who can relieve her of the burden of solitude. She has, as a matter of fact, reached breaking point. At the same time she is weighed down by a feeling of her own worthlessness, partly instilled into her by her stepfather's critical attitude to her accomplishments as a lady. The strange lady, who, she soon discovers, is rich and independent, takes on the colouring of an ideal. She is, to some extent, what Elizabeth-Jane would like to be. At least she represents freedom and escape.

Later on one feels that Lucetta exploits her friend, completely stealing the show from her. However unconsciously, she gradually takes on the role of glamorous rival, who eventually destroys Elizabeth-Jane's chance of happiness. But the passage which describes their first meeting shows that Elizabeth's role from then on as foil to the leading beauty of the town is partly self-imposed. She tones herself down and projects what little she has of social ambition on to Lucetta – or does she already anticipate that her own, at least potential, social position will be usurped anyway by the newcomer? Jealousy is never overtly expressed, but there is a hint of it in the information that 'she felt all the freshness and grace to be stolen from herself . . .'

There is always something ephemeral about Lucetta's beauty. She stands out against the 'honest homeliness which mostly prevailed' in Casterbridge (p. 136). Returning home, Elizabeth-Jane muses 'on what she had seen, as she might have mused on a rainbow or the Northern Lights, a rare butterfly or a cameo' (p. 136). All these are wonders, well outside the world of the beholder. It would seem, however, that the 'rare butterfly' is the most revealing part of her reflection.

As Lucetta's companion at High Place Hall, she is supposed to act as a kind of chaperone during the expected visits from Henchard. But finding that she is in love with Farfrae and that Henchard hates his stepdaughter, Lucetta instead uses her friend as a watchdog to keep the latter away.

From now on the two ladies are inseparable. It is, however, always clear that Elizabeth-Jane is there merely to set off Lucetta's beauty and elegance, and otherwise keep in the background as much as possible. Lucetta may not be entirely aware of the use she makes of her companion. Neither is it clear how far the role of foil, on Elizabeth's part, is self-assumed. But again Hardy's fondness for the pictorial method emphasizes the effect of absolute contrasts which the High Place Hall chapters produce.

At the height of this section the two women are confronted with one another in a dress scene. Lucetta is trying on two new dresses that have arrived from London, attended by Elizabeth-Jane. Lucetta's glamourousness is thrown into high relief, but so is her superficiality. She is shown studying '[t]he gowns spread out on the bed . . . in an attitude of contemplation' (p. 167). Elizabeth-Jane's remark, ' "I wouldn't think so hard about it" ' (p. 167), is very revealing. She knows what contemplation means. Lucetta's greatest mental problem appears to be choosing new apparel: she complains, ' ". . . settling upon new clothes is so trying" ' (p. 167).

Lucetta's attention is switched from clothes to a glamorous event in the marketplace. A new agricultural machine has arrived, and the two women go down to admire it. Anticipating that she might meet Farfrae, Lucetta decides to wear her 'new attire', while Elizabeth-Jane, almost pointedly it seems, 'pitchfork[s] on' her 'bonnet and shawl' (p. 168). The contrast between them could not have been more striking. The sexual implications of the scene become clear when the women meet Farfrae. Although Elizabeth-Jane does most of the talking, he is hardly aware of her at all. His attention is riveted by Lucetta. '. . . Farfrae appeared only conscious of [Lucetta]. . .' (p. 170).

At times Lucetta's concern with the surface of things takes on an hysterical tone, particularly when her own situation as a woman is involved. This is very evident in the scene in which Elizabeth-Jane is asked to bring a looking-glass so that Lucetta may scrutinize her own features and assess the way she appears to other people. The mirror and the emphasis on appearance suggest a dress-image, which is further indicated in a later question, ' "I wonder if I wear well, as times go!" ' (p. 174). Her remark and the conversation that follows bring out Lucetta's anxiety about appearance, and her hysterical fear that her youth and beauty will fade before she has achieved 'happiness' through marriage. She uses Elizabeth-Jane both as a foil to set off her elegance and as a sort of guarantee that she will not be overtaken by time. The incident, however, also shows that Lucetta may be regarded as a foil to Elizabeth-Jane, whose superior moral and intellectual worth is brought out by the former's social superficiality.

Lucetta's and Farfrae's marriage terminates Elizabeth-Jane's stay at

High Place Hall. On her departure she almost ceremonially '[takes] off her pretty dress and array[s] herself in a plain one . . .' (p. 217). The action severs her link with Lucetta and puts an end to her role as foil. But the contrast she offers to her is important even at that moment. While Lucetta lives in constant fear of her past because it may erupt and ruin her social and sexual position, Elizabeth-Jane never dreams of denying her past. She is always prepared to return to the poverty that to Pamela is a feared, though at times tempting possibility. Elizabeth-Jane's plain dress, like her pattens, is always available, not to parade her humility in, but as her firm hold on reality. Her plainness may have a touch of narrow-mindedness, but it is above all emblematic of her uprightness, integrity, and sense of values.

The possession of an 'inner chamber of ideas', at least as real to her as external reality – 'visible objects' (p. 98) – distinguishes Elizabeth-Jane from all the other characters in the novel. She is provided with the kind of hidden reserves that enable her to withstand the buffetings of fortune better than they do, with the possible exception of Farfrae. The inner world of her mind is a storehouse of potentialities, within which there is room for moral and intellectual development. She possesses certain basic qualities from the start, like reticence, meekness, sobriety, '. . . a willingness to sacrifice her personal comfort and dignity to the common weal' (p. 47), and, above all, patient endurance. Her conservative sense of loyalty is combined with 'circumspection' and 'an innate perceptiveness that [is] almost genius' (p. 90).

The feature that most markedly distinguishes Elizabeth-Jane from the other characters is her insatiable thirst for knowledge, combined with perseverance. On her first appearance we are told 'how zealously and constantly the young mind . . . [is] struggling for enlargement . . . The desire . . . of Elizabeth-Jane's heart [is] . . . to see, to hear, and to understand' (p. 30). When her fortunes change, and the town has started to take notice of her, Elizabeth-Jane cautions herself: ' "There is something wrong in all this . . . If they only knew what an unfinished girl I am . . . Better sell all this finery and buy myself grammar-books and dictionaries and a history of all the philosophies!" ' (p. 99).

There is a strong bent towards the scholar in Elizabeth-Jane's nature, part of her introvert, reflective temperament. Clothes and the art of dressing well are accomplishments she has to learn because of her new social position. But the world of books is far more important to her. She works hard to get rid of her provincialism to please her stepfather, but above all 'she read[s] omnivorously' (p. 131). The ordeal Henchard submits her to is both cruel and unjust. It seems to her, who does not know the real reason for his changed behaviour, that '[t]he more interesting that her appearance and manners became under the softening influences which she could now command, and in her wisdom did command, the more she seemed to estrange him' (133). The lonely girl in her solitary chamber is a pathetic sight, but her perseverance turns her rom into an outpost of learning:

She read and took notes incessantly, mastering facts with painful laboriousness, but never flinching from her self-imposed task. She began the study of Latin, incited by the Roman characteristics of the town she lived in (p. 134).

Her studies may be said to be futile and useless since they can only be a means of achieving self-improvement. But in the long run they help to build up the spiritual resources she amasses, in contrast to the others, who are bent on wordly success. Her painful studies make her intensely aware of her intellectual shortcomings. Thus we are told that 'Elizabeth's mind [runs] on acquirements to an almost morbid degree' (p. 153). She is therefore naively impressed by Lucetta's knowledge of French. It is natural, Elizabeth-Jane feels, that such an accomplished lady should be skilled in languages. The learning she has acquired from books, is, however, joined to her natural wisdom and capacity for deep thinking and reflection. Towards the end of the book we are told that the sadness of her thoughts on the occasion of Lucetta's death 'added charm to a countenance whose beauty had ever lain in its meditative soberness' (p. 294).

One of Elizabeth's main roles is that of commentator on life and events. She is well equipped for this role by her studious and meditative temperament and her unusual awareness of the harshness and unpredictability of fate. Her pessimistic reflections on the impossibility that Farfrae should care for her take on a general tone. Looking at herself in the mirror, 'Elizabeth thought . . . that by this time he had discovered how plain and homely was the informing spirit of that pretty outside' (p. 114). But more typical is the sort of reflection she makes during the night she watches over her dying mother: '. . . all this while the subtle-souled girl asking herself why she was born, why sitting in a room, and blinking at the candle; why things around her had taken the shape they wore in preference to every other possible shape' (p. 121). She goes on to ask a number of questions that touch on the riddle of existence.[19] Profound pessimism is at the core of her stoicism.

Experience has taught Elizabeth-Jane 'the lesson of renunciation, and [she is] as familiar with the wreck of each day's wishes as with the diurnal setting of the sun' (pp. 179–180). The position she gains by marrying Farfrae, gives her the opportunity of 'discovering to the narrow-lived ones around her the secret . . . of making limited opportunities endurable . . .' (p. 333). Although she is fully aware of 'those minute forms of satisfaction that offer themselves to everybody not in positive pain . . .', she is nevertheless convinced that 'happiness [is] but the occasional episode in a general drama of pain' (p. 334). These are the final words in the book. The language is that of the narrator. The views expressed are, however, the sum of Elizabeth-Jane's experience and her career as observer of the human condition, ruled by the law of 'flux and reflux'.[20]

The latter is perhaps the most important function Elizabeth-Jane is made to serve in the novel. She is throughout a 'sensitive consciousness',[21] who watches and reflects. All her other roles coalesce in the role of observer. Elizabeth-Jane is at once inside and outside the experience she records and comments on. She cannot avoid being touched by life – at least as a victim. The passivity inherent in the role of woman is an important element in the observer's stance – she is, by nature, doomed to be a looker-on rather than an active participant.

Arriving in Casterbridge in the company of Elizabeth-Jane and her mother, we are invited to see the ancient town through the girl's young and inexperienced eyes. Everything is new and fresh to her, and she takes in everything – scenery, shop windows, people, and events – with absorbed interest. The narrator does not specify her experience of the scene. He merely puts her in the middle of it, as in the account of her walk through the bustling town to Henchard's house, on the first morning of her stay in the town. Towards the end of the sketch Elizabeth-Jane's viewpoint is introduced, contrasted with that of the experienced and mature narrator:

All the venerable contrivances and confusions which delighted the eye by their quaintness, and in a measure reasonableness, in this rare old market-town, were metropolitan novelties to the unpractised eyes of Elizabeth-Jane, fresh from netting fish-seines in a sea-side cottage (p. 66).

The girl's limited experience is made clear, but also the freshness of her approach, which suffuses the initial passages about Casterbridge with a particular atmosphere of excitement.

Elizabeth-Jane has, however, already been confronted with what are to be the main forces that shape her existence, the main components of the pattern of experience that is to turn her into a mature woman. The night before, as one of the outsiders, she had first seen Henchard in all his glory, and then Farfrae, at that point as much of an outsider as she is. Hillis Miller draws attention to Hardy's 'emphasis on seeing as the chief way a man is related to others . . .'[22] This is well documented in the first scene in which Elizabeth-Jane's role as observer is fully revealed.

On her first evening in Casterbridge she joins the crowd outside the hotel in order to discover Henchard's circumstances. Through the open window of the hotel she has her first view of the man who is to play such a central part in her life. The window is from now on closely linked with her role as observer. In this scene it focuses on the social structure of the town. The Mayor and his guests form the hierarchy of the community, surrounded by the populace, who, like the chorus of a Greek tragedy, watches and comments.

At the same time the window suggests a scrutinizing eye which can detect the features and characteristic behaviour of those inside. The mother's viewpoint – determined by her recognition of the Mayor as her husband – is added to that of Elizabeth-Jane, who, unaware of the truth, is merely surprised when she discovers that they are 'akin to a coach' (p. 38). This discovery, and the novelty of the scene as a whole, make her feel that she has 'never been so much interested in anything in her life as in their present position ...' (p. 38). The 'picture' is gradually filled in by the bystanders, who comment on Henchard's outstanding career: ' "He worked his way up from nothing when 'a came here; and now he's a pillar of the town" ' (p. 40).

The theme of change and mutability, of central importance in the novel, is in the foreground in this remark. It hovers in the background when the completely unknown Scotsman, merely a knight of fortune, turns up outside the window and sends in the note which starts his relationship with Henchard. Elizabeth-Jane watches the incident.

Not a sound comes through the window. It is as if the two sets of people live in completely separated worlds.[23] They can watch each other, but communication or interference is impossible. Elizabeth-Jane observes the Mayor's face as he reads Farfrae's letter, struck by the contrast between him and the other guests. Their increasing conviviality is shown in a sort of pantomime, in which 'Henchard ... remain[s] stately and vertical, silently thinking' (p. 43).

Throughout the novel Elizabeth-Jane is provided with a vantage point from which she can view her surroundings. The observation post may be inherent in the job she happens to be doing. This is the case when she works as a waiting maid at the inn where she and her mother are staying, in order to eke out their scant means. She is enabled to hear and watch the goings-on in the parlour. Her obscure position partly explains Farfrae's unawareness of her, while his singing and general behaviour attract her to him from the beginning. While she serves him in his room, next door to their own, he almost ignores her. She can therefore look at him 'quite coolly' (p. 48). The following portrait of the young man seems completely impersonal, but the eyes that see are Elizabeth-Jane's, and there is a touch of admiration in the lingering attention to every line and feature in the man's face. One is made to feel that despite the spectator's detachment, this is the moment when the girl starts to care for Farfrae. Watching the company in the parlour later in the evening, she perceives a spiritual kinship with him and is struck by the difference between him and the others:

She admired the serious light in which he looked at serious things. ... He seemed to feel exactly as she felt about life and its surroundings – that they were a tragical

64

rather than a comical thing; that though one could be gay on occasion, moments of gaiety were interludes, and no part of the actual drama (p. 59).

The passage demonstrates the way Elizabeth-Jane combines the roles of observer and commentator. Her clear vision goes beyond the external scene to the underlying values and principles. Her usual channel of involvement is general reflection which links the particular with the universal.

From now on the window tends to be Elizabeth-Jane's favourite observation post, enabling her to watch life as it passes by with detachment and clarity of vision. From the window in her room at the inn she sees Farfrae and Henchard walk up the street on the morning the former intends to leave for America. Her view takes in the wide prospect of town and country and shows how closely the two are integrated. At first the voices of the two men can be heard, but the main effect of the scene is that of a picture. As they vanish out of sight, Farfrae and Henchard seem 'small as two grains of corn ...' (p. 62). The long view has reduced them to a proportion that harmonizes with their surroundings; Nature has put them in their place. The long view reduces everything to microscopical details – human beings as well.

In her stepfather's house Elizabeth-Jane is given a back-room, overlooking the yard. From her window she can act the role of 'silent observing woman' (p. 113). She witnesses the rise and fall of the friendship between her stepfather and the Scotsman. Watching them in the yard below, she is continually assessing their behaviour and displaying her understanding of their natures:

Her quiet eye discerned that Henchard's tigerish affection for the younger man, his constant liking to have Farfrae near him, now and then resulted in a tendency to domineer, which, however, was checked in a moment when Donald exhibited marks of real offence (p. 93).

Her clear view enables her to penetrate below the surface and interpret. Her 'quiet eye' sees both action and motive with intuitive insight.

The window provides the 'optical detachment' which Hillis Miller notes in the role of the 'spectator narrator' in Hardy's novels.[24] The incisive force of the view from a point that is sufficiently detached from that of the characters viewed to provide perspective and a sense of proportion, is evident in the passage which records the climax of the friendship between Henchard and Farfrae:

She looked from the window and saw Henchard and Farfrae in the hay-yard talking, with that impetuous cordiality on the Mayor's part, and genial modesty on the younger man's, that was now so generally observable in their intercourse. Friendship between man and man; what a rugged strength there was in it, as evinced by these two. And yet the seed that was to lift the foundation of this friendship was at that moment taking root in a chink of its structure (p. 99).

65

Then follows the confrontation between the two men over Abel Whittle, the beginning of the process that disrupts their friendship and leads to Henchard's destruction.

The passage is, first of all, a cool and factual account of what Elizabeth-Jane sees in the yard. Gradually, however, the 'picture' recedes, and the commentator takes over, combining assessment with general reflection. The emphasis on the absolute contrast between the two men is followed by praise of friendship between 'man and man'. The words are the narrator's, but as the viewpoint is Elizabeth-Jane's, one may perhaps detect a note of wistful envy: as a woman she is barred from this kind of emotional experience. On the other hand, the final sentence hints that nothing in the field of human experience can remain perfect; there is always 'a chink in its structure.'

The most important instance of detached insight is contained in the concluding sentence. It is slightly ambiguous, again owing to the circumstance that we see with Elizabeth-Jane's eyes, but do not listen to her voice. The narrator warns us what is going to happen. But the force of the statement probably derives from the illusion which is created that we, the readers, are enabled, through Elizabeth-Jane, to watch the very moment when the 'seed' takes root in the 'chink'. We are able to detect the flaw as well as the beginning of the destructive process. In addition, through the long view of the narrator, we are given a glimpse of the far-reaching consequences of this particular moment.

The final note of unavoidable fate is stressed by the use of a detached, but not indifferent observer. Elizabeth-Jane can, from her window, see what is happening, at least anticipating the inevitable consequences of the moment. But she is unable to interfere in any way. It is the curse of the 'silent observing woman' that her tongue is tied. She can see, but not warn.

Elizabeth-Jane may be said to act like a barometer,[25] recording the fluctuating relationship and long-drawn-out rivalry between Farfrae and Henchard, but from an increasing distance, owing to her stepfather's coolness towards her and his ban on her friendship with his competitor. When Farfrae leaves Henchard's employment, she moves to a front room, overlooking the street. Her window provides her with little comfort: '. . . as for the young man, whenever he passed the house he seldom or never turned his head' (p. 135). Her role as observer accentuates that of victim. She watches, as it were, from behind the bars of her prison.

At first Elizabeth-Jane's friendship with Lucetta is a change for the better. This is reflected in the two girl's fondness for the glorious view of the bustling market-place from the window. On the other hand, the view from the window also highlights the pre-determined nature of existence. The market-place is the heart of the community; the setting for its most vital transactions. The square is compared to 'the regular Open Place in spectacular dramas, where the incidents that occur always happen to bear on the lives of the adjoining residents' (p. 166). The remark illuminates the dramatic structure of the novel.[26] The struggle between Farfrae and Henchard for commercial and sexual supremacy is watched and 'felt' by all the other characters, by Elizabeth-Jane in particular. She is, as we have seen, pushed more and more into the background, but she does not relinquish her position as observer of a drama that concerns her so much, but in which she is reduced to the roles of mutely suffering spectator and foil. Hillis Miller observes the way Hardy's 'watchers at a distance ... are almost always infatuated with another person. Their watching has a focus.'[27]

All along we have been aware of Elizabeth-Jane's 'focus', but in the window-scenes in the High Place Hall chapters her partiality for Farfrae is so much in the foreground that it almost obscures the clarity of her vision. A complication is of course her incomplete knowledge of what is going on.

The moment she is undeceived, Elizabeth-Jane is again given the observer's sharp vision. Characteristically, knowledge is what restores it: 'A seer's spirit took possession of Elizabeth, impelling her to sit down by the fire and divine events so surely from data already her own that they could be held as witnessed' (p. 172). There is not the faintest hint that she is thinking of putting up a fight; she merely withdraws quietly into the private world of her mind: 'She stoically looked from her bedroom window, and contemplated her fate as if it were written on the top of the church-tower hard by' (p. 175). The window emphasizes the detachment with which she views herself – and others. The completeness of her withdrawal is revealed when she witnesses the ritual duel which Henchard and Farfrae fight over a cup of tea in Lucetta's drawing room. '... from the crystalline sphere of a straightforward mind ...' (p. 179) the hopelessness as well as the absurdity of the rivalry appear clearly. Once more she is the silent observer who suffers, but does not warn.

The room to which Elizabeth-Jane moves after her rupture with Lucetta, is a prison cell compared with High Place Hall. She spends her days netting and studying (p. 227). From her window she can 'see Donald and Lucetta speeding in and out of their door with all the bounding enthusiasm of their situation' (pp. 227–8). She stoically tries to avoid the view as well as their company, apparently completely reduced to a background character.

However, as Henchard's fortunes decline, the moment inevitably approaches when he will need her. We are told that she 'kept her eye' upon him (p. 236). Sitting by her window one Sunday she discovers he has started drinking again (p. 230). Ready enough to help him, she is nevertheless mainly a passive observer. Her habitual response to life is shown up during the Royal Visit, during which Henchard makes his last effort to assert himself in the community of Casterbridge. Elizabeth-Jane is one of the spectators. Although she has by now assumed care and responsibility for her stepfather, it soon becomes clear how tied she is to her observation post. When she realizes what he is up to, she is 'terrified', but '... then her interest in the spectacle as a strange phenomenon [gets] the better of her fear' (p. 266). There is a noncommital streak in her character. Her unwillingness to become involved is perhaps an inevitable consequence of her buffeting by fate.

One of our last glimpses of Elizabeth-Jane reveals her in her favourite position by the window. Her newly recovered father and Farfrae are discussing Henchard's conduct and plans for her imminent wedding. Elizabeth remains silent. Newson requests her to 'come and hearken to what [they are talking] about, and not bide staring out o' the window as if she didn't hear' (p. 314). Elizabeth tells them that she leaves everything to them, 'still keeping up a scrutinizing gaze at some small object in the street' (p. 315). She is once more absorbed in her own private world, which throughout has been her bulwark against a hostile universe. Only Newson's account of Henchard's deception can wrench her out of her detachment. She makes her most explicit statement in the whole novel when she denounces her stepfather: ' "I said I would never forget him. But O! I think I ought to forget him now!" ' (p. 316).

It is part of the ironical pattern of the novel that even a clear-sighted character like Elizabeth-Jane can be cruel and unjust because she does not possess full knowledge. This is a common experience, and it is one of Elizabeth-Jane's functions to illustrate the human lot. We have seen that there is a gulf between the god-like omniscience displayed by the narrator and the after all limited knowledge of a character like Elizabeth-Jane. She acts as a bridge between the narrator and the human world he portrays. But it is also clear that he approaches her in exactly the same way as any other character. He uses her eyes, but he rarely uses her tongue. She, too, is viewed from a considerable distance. He alternately furnishes her with and bars her from knowledge. We have seen examples of her penetrating insight. At other times she does not see what is right in front of her, or the narrator deliberately makes her miss something that would have been of considerable importance to her. An example of the latter is when Farfrae calls during her absence and is won by Lucetta instead. An example of the former is the 'meeting' between Henchard and Elizabeth-Jane in the alley behind High Place Hall. She does not want to be seen, so she hides when she hears someone coming up the street. As a result they are unaware of each other's presence. Had they seen each other, the course of events might well have been different.

The narrator's favourite approach is, as we have seen, pictorial. He combines the long view with microscopic scrutiny. Again and again he places the foreground – city, village, individual characters – against the background of a vast landscape of space and time.[28] At times the emptiness of the scene suggests a newly created world, but when man appears he is a pathetic rather than a hopeful figure. This is poignantly expressed at the beginning of the novel in the picture of Henchard and his young family trudging along the dreary road. It is even more in the foreground during Henchard's last journey across the strangely empty Wessex landscape.

There is no question of man conquering the space of which he forms such an insignificant part. It is rather that he is dwarfed or crushed by it. The vast perspective is the author's way of facing what he sees as reality with unflinching honesty.

The tendency to subject details to intense scrutiny is particularly striking when the object under investigation is man. Hardy is fond of astronomical images, which fix man in an unalterable course. An apparently innocent phrase like 'centre of gravity' (p. 126) becomes meaningful when applied to Elizabeth-Jane, because one has throughout such a vivid impression that she is imprisoned within a narrow sphere. The information that she has 'changed her orbit from one of gay independence to laborious self-help . . .' (p. 144) has a similar effect. The girl's dependence on others is accentuated, as well as the limited, monotonous nature of her existence.

The effect of the narrator's coldly scrutinizing technique is particularly striking when the human face is submitted to investigation. Not only does the analyser expose every crease and every angle, he also seems to assume that the face may reveal a pre-set pattern. Thus the face of the sleeping Elizabeth-Jane indicates 'buried genealogical facts, ancestral curves, dead men's traits . . .' (p. 128). It is as if the individual carries the dead of past generations with him and in sleep returns to them. The 'statuesque repose of the young girl's countenance . . .' (p. 128) is indistinguishable from rigor mortis. The skeleton, the planned outline, is visible in the young, unformed face, exposed by the sun:

Her face, though somewhat wan and incomplete, possessed the raw materials of beauty in a promising degree. There was an under-handsomeness in it, struggling to reveal itself through the provisional curves of immaturity . . . She was handsome in the bone, hardly as yet handsome in the flesh. She possibly might never be fully handsome, unless the carking accidents of daily existence could be evaded before the mobile parts of her countenance had settled to their final mould (p. 30).

This long quotation illustrates the author's obsession on the one hand with the indestructible element in the human face – curve, shape, bone – on the other with the process of becoming, the brief moment before the face has become fixed and set, almost like a living corpse. In a previous passage the girl has been shown to possess the 'ephemeral precious essence youth . . .' (p. 24), while '. . . life's middle summer had set its hardening mark on the mother's face . . .' (p. 24). Elizabeth-Jane is the replica of her mother as a young girl.

The method resembles that of an archaeologist who carefully uncovers a skeleton. There is indeed a continual endeavour to unearth the relics of the distant past in *The Mayor of Casterbridge*. The skeletons that are found at times appear almost as alive as the present inhabitants, as in the following account of the position in which they were usually found:

> It was impossible to dig . . . without coming upon some tall soldier . . . who had lain there in his silent unobtrusive rest for a space of fifteen hundred years. He was mostly found lying on his side, in an oval scoop in the chalk, like a chicken in its shell; his knees drawn up to his chest . . . (p. 73).

If the sleeping girl looked as though she were dead, the skeleton is described as though it were asleep. The same scrutinizing approach has been used.

Hardy's method of presenting his world is so inhuman and impersonal that a softening subsidiary viewpoint is required. The limitations set for this viewpoint are severe. Elizabeth-Jane's case offers ample evidence. She is made to share, in the main, her creator's outlook, but, unlike him, she has to descend into the world of his characters and share their conditions. She is given very little scope and independence. Yet one may agree with H. C. Webster's view:

> Although her negative excellences do not win for her as much admiration as Henchard's positive virtues and vices, Elizabeth Jane unquestionably illustrates a practical way of making the best of things as they are.[29]

The solution seems trivial, and in the vast context of Hardy's void of a universe it seems absurd. It is, however, Elizabeth-Jane's function to make us see the true nature of existence, while persuading us that although life may seem insupportable, stoic acceptance is still a workable solution. Moreover, her stoicism is a considered view of life, an awareness she has reached after much suffering. It is therefore evidence of her humanity and spiritual resilience, evidence of both the bleakness and the invincibility of the human condition.

CHAPTER IV

E. M. Forster, *A Passage to India.*
Accent and Design

The three previous chapters have shown three aspects of the art of persuasion and its impact on the various elements in the language of fiction: overt didactic purpose, the pattern formed by certain recurrent features, the use made of a particular character. In *A Passage to India* one is struck by the effect achieved through design and accent, the 'tonal' emphasis the author achieves through modulations of point of view. This is the 'power to expand and contract perception . . . [the] right to intermittent knowledge' E. M. Forster claims as 'one of the greatest advantages of the novel form . . .'[1]

In his introduction to the volume of critical essays on *A Passage to India* in the Casebook series Malcolm Bradbury declares that 'few other novels have produced such a *variety* of reading and emphasis, such a critical multiplicity of opinion'. Critics as well as readers may focus on particular aspects of the novel, to the exclusion of others.[2]

June Perry Levine in her book *Creation and Criticism. A Passage to India,* presents a survey of the criticism of the novel which shows how diverse and even contradictory its reception has been. As regards themes she finds 'two main areas of opinion – that the novel represents either a positive vision of love, order, and unity or a negative vision of despair, chaos, and separation . . .'[3] This kind of emphasis may have a labelling effect and is too narrow, perhaps even misleading. Forster's novel is the result of an art which juxtaposes even irreconcilable contrasts and mysteriously unites them into a whole which transcends the parts. Forster, like Coleridge in 'Kubla Khan', has built a 'sunny pleasure-dome with caves of ice', and somehow the question of whether the sun or the ice is more important is minor compared to the miracle of the dome, which transcends both.

Alan Wilde draws attention to

... the feeling, which is apparent to some degree in all the fiction, that life is fundamentally disordered, that at its very foundations the universe is chaotic. It is a feeling that explains why the search for order motivates and dominates Forster's thought and why ... it becomes the leading theme of the later fiction.[4]

71

All art is the imposition of form on chaos; the artist is a creator. June Perry Levine discusses E. M. Forster's view that art ' "creates little worlds of its own, possessing internal harmony, in the bosom of this disordered planet." '[5] In a novel like *A Passage to India* one is continually aware of the author's vision of the abyss which surrounds both the world he has created and the 'reality' from which it arose. Like Hardy he places the world of men in a vast, non-human universe, which makes his own effort at formal perfection paradoxical. If chaos is the 'natural' condition, and meaninglessness the barrier we cannot surmount, the idea of art as a means of taming the wilderness may not seem to make sense. Is art child's play, the web of illusion, or is it man's supreme defiance of the unknown, his main access to ultimate truth?

If the novel is approached in terms of emphasis, no one area of meaning need be singled out. Each one is relevant, as it was put into the novel to guide the reader's response. This somewhat naive statement alludes to the obvious fact that everything in the novel is designed, minor details as well as larger elements. The world of art is an artefact, designed and constructed by the novelist, who, like the architect, displays sure technical skill and a sure eye for the total artistic effect of his work. This is strikingly evident in a novel like *A Passage to India*, in which concern with form is so apparent. Both the texture and the structure of the novel demonstrate the manner in which the author, by modulating the emphasis he brings to bear upon his material, achieves the remarkable synthesis of clarity and complexity which the novel represents. Emphasis is a question of design, and above all of accent, of intellectual and emotional tone, all the varied and complex ways in which pressure is brought to bear upon the reader.

The opening chapter of the novel introduces a number of strata that run through the whole novel. The vast panorama of the novel is outlined. The long view seems to include the whole of India. At the same time the elemental aspects of the setting are singled out for lingering attention: earth/rock, river, sky. The author's concern with the elemental is linked with an urge to seek back to the 'origin' of the world which surrounds the community he is about to describe. The city of Chandrapore consists of layers of human existence, ranging from the civil station through the native city which, as it stretches down to the river, moves closer and closer to 'mud' – the lowest level of human existence. This part of the city is seen as the 'excrescence' which the river 'might be expected to wash ... back into the soil' (p. 9).[6] It is compared to 'some low but indestructible form of life' (p. 9). The Marabar Hills dominate the horizon. The 'endless expanse' (p. 11) suggests infinite space as well as time. The image of the hills as 'fists and fingers ... thrust up through the soil ...' (p. 11) carries, in addition to connotations of aggression and force, an undertone of creative eruption. This is as far back as one can get. Before the Marabar Hills rose, the 'expanse' was truly endless – like the pre-creation void.

In the passage in which this image occurs, the suggestion of a movement back to the barely imaginable beginning is joined with the idea of a cosmic process. The sky is seen as the one feature that can unite the elements of the Chandrapore setting. Like the other features in the landscape, it is personified:

> The sky settles everything ... when the sky chooses, glory can rain into the Chandrapore bazaars or a benediction pass from horizon to horizon. The sky can do this because it is so strong and so enormous. Strength comes from the sun, infused in it daily, size from the prostrate earth. No mountains infringe on the curve. League after league the earth lies flat, heaves a little, is flat again. Only in the south ... (pp. 10–11).

and then comes the reference to the caves.

It is as if the Hills and the caves were, at a particular moment beyond human memory, born as a result of the union between the sun and the earth, or perhaps the void of the endless sky. We are in the realm of myth,[7] which persists as an undertone throughout the novel, but comes to the fore from time to time.

In Chapter 12, the first chapter of the Caves section, myth dominates completely. Again there is a suggestion of a fruitful union between the sun and the earth: 'If flesh of the sun's flesh is to be touched anywhere, it is here, among the incredible antiquity of these hills' (p. 123). The emphasis on a miraculous interruption of the endless flow of time is deepened in the reference to the almost unimaginable future when 'an ocean will flow here too, and cover the sun-born rocks with slime' (p. 123).

The background of the vast landscape in Chapter 1 dwarfs the human element, as it does in *The Mayor of Casterbridge* and *The Return of the Native*. This effect is further emphasized by the absence of human individuals in this chapter. We are only introduced to the man-made landscape, the city of Chandrapore, an outcrop of the non-human universe.

Within the landscape shaped by man contrast is a ruling principle. Native Chandrapore, mean, filthy, decaying, slum-like, seems a completely different world from that of the civil station, well-planned, clean, luxurious – a 'city of gardens'.

It is interesting to see how emphasis is a matter of accent in these passages. The opening sentence of the chapter strikes a casual, 'guidebook' note,[8] which implies that the Caves, unlike Chandrapore, are 'extraordinary'. The emphasis is on 'nothing' – the absence of uniqueness and vitality. Even the implication that the Caves are 'extraordinary' is qualified: 'they are twenty miles off ...' (p. 9), and therefore out of reach. Is it distance that makes them interesting? In the course of the novel it becomes clear that it is by no means easy to make the label 'extraordinary' stick to them.

The negative element persists right through the description of the native city: 'There are no bathing-steps on the river front, as the Ganges happens not to be holy here; indeed there is no river front . . . Chandrapore was never large or beautiful . . .' (p. 9). It is a deprived city: '. . . bazaars shut out the wide and shifting panorama of the stream. The streets are mean, the temples ineffective . . .' (p. 9). The few beautiful houses are tucked away in gardens, and 'filth deters all but the invited guest. . . . There is no painting and scarely any carving in the bazaars' (p. 9). The town's only possession seems to be 'mud', symbolizing mere existence.

The civil station, by contrast, is at first described in terms of its possessions: 'On the second rise is laid out the little civil station . . . It is a city of gardens. It is no city, but a forest sparsely scattered with huts. It is a tropical pleasaunce washed by a noble river' (p. 9). The recurrent 'it is' emphasizes its order and tidiness. It can easily be defined and outlined. But 'it is' also suggests the aggressiveness of this community, its insistence on being a 'fact'. The deceptiveness of the position of the civil station is hinted at in the description of the view. Native Chandrapore 'appears to be a totally different place' (p. 9) when viewed from the station. Distance, as in the case of the Hills, is a distorting factor. Further, the huge trees that fill the gardens act as a screen against the city, but also 'glorify' it, so that newcomers experience disillusionment when they visit the actual town. In addition, the ancient trees dwarf the civil station: '. . . endowed with more strength than man or his works, they soar above the lower deposit to greet one another with branches and beckoning leaves, and to build a city for the birds' (p. 10).[9]

Finally, the civil station is described in a passage which moves from negation, through 'it is', to a final negation of any link between the Anglo-Indian quarters and their surroundings, except the view and the sky. We are prepared for the cosmic vision of the final paragraphs:

As for the civil station itself, it provokes no emotion. It charms not, neither does it repel. It is sensibly planned, with a red-brick club on its brow, and farther back a grocer's and a cemetery, and the bungalows are disposed along roads that intersect at right angles. It has nothing hideous in it, and only the view is beautiful; it shares nothing with the city except the overarching sky (p. 10).

The lack of emotion mentioned at the beginning of the quotation is reflected in the passage as a whole. Everything is neat and well planned – at 'right angles', in a context where nothing is tidy or well planned. The network of roads symbolizes 'the imposed, the intellectual, the unnatural order that the British have manufactured in India . . .'[10] '[N]oth-ing' turns even 'hideous' into a virtue, and the beautiful view is, as we have seen, an illusion, or, like the sky, 'overarching' and therefore out of reach.

The guidebook opening has an ironic undertone in two ways. It creates a sense of expectation that is not fulfilled. Also, the account of the native city is not of the kind you would expect to find in a guide-book, stressing as it does the trivial, unromantic aspects of the town. In fact, the author appears to play down any element that the tourist might have found picturesque. The language itself is flat, unemotional, factual, in striking contrast to the colourful language of the final passages, in which the non-human elements of the setting are described. As a matter of fact, as soon as the author leaves the human scene and moves towards the setting, he becomes less casual, as when he describes the way the native city mingles with its background, or the forest that defies and ignores the encroachments of the civil station.

Bradbury writes about 'two tones that come into perplexing relation-ship [in the novel]. There is the instinct towards "poetry" . . . and there is the comedy and the irony, the belittling aspect of his tone . . .'[11] Al-though there is no dialogue in Chapter 1, the narrator nevertheless re-veals the width of his scope, spanning as it does the two 'tones' as well as the range of nuances between them. Much of the appeal of the novel depends on the emphasis the author achieves by shifting rapidly and often unobtrusively between the symbolic, grand style of the poet and prophet and the casual, common-sense style of the humane, detached social critic.

The first chapter sets the perspective; the following chapters focus our attention on the characters that fill the stage, with a whole continent as a backcloth. The narrative is interspersed with dialogue and authorial commentary and description.

Chapter 2 opens in a light-hearted mood. After briefly revealing the youth, carelessness, and impulsive warmth of the newcomer, Dr. Aziz, we are shown him bandying words with his friends. When they tell him that they are having 'a very sad talk' (p. 12), he does not appear to believe them, and neither do we. He is next shown in a paradisical situation, serenely smoking on the veranda: 'Delicious indeed to lie on the broad veranda with the moon rising in front and the servants preparing dinner behind, and no trouble happening' (p. 12).

Seen against such a background the sad talk does not appear very sad. The subject of their argument – 'whether or not it is possible to be friends with an Englishman' (p. 12) – seems strangely theoretical. It is, however, one of the main themes of the novel, the backbone of the plot pattern. It is important to see that at this stage neither of the speakers feels very strongly on the subject. Although they cannot quote a single instance of such friendship outside England, they are not really bitter about it, their mood being generally benevolent. Further, they appear to put forward views and standpoints as the spirit moves them, playing on a wide range of feeling, from optimism and the desire to prove that friendship is possible, to irony and scepticism. Their knowledge of the way the 'system' forms every Englishman and makes him reject any personal link with the Indians, is combined with their susceptibility to rumours of any kind, for example that their rulers take bribes. Aziz takes little interest in the discussion, even suggesting that the question need not arise: ' "Why talk about the English? ... Why be either friends with the fellows or not friends? Let us shut them out and be jolly" ' (p. 14), echoing the ancient poetry of which he is so fond. Again their mood changes, and we see them straining their memories to recall 'little kindnesses and courtesies' (p. 14) shown them by the English.

Both before and during dinner Aziz and his friends drift from mood to mood, and from subject to subject – marriage, mere teasing, poetry – and to each subject they surrender wholeheartedly. Little of this is rendered in dialogue form. The narrator is always ready to summarize, interpret, and comment. The theme of friendship is presented in a kind of aside. Aziz is shown enjoying his leisure and his pipe. The characters, their talk, and the subject of their talk pass through the filter of narrative and implied attitude:

He lay in a trance, sensuous but healthy, through which the talk of the two others did not seem particularly sad – they were discussing [the theme of friendship between the races]. Mahmoud Ali argued that it was not, Hamidullah disagreed, but with so many reservations that there was no friction between them (p. 12).

We are given the impression of listening to their talk, but we are also provided with an angle which facilitates sympathetic insight. A certain cool detachment is nevertheless retained.

Such a filter is perceived throughout the chapter. When the host shouts for dinner, the '[s]ervants shouted back that it was ready. They meant that they wished it was ready, and were so understood, for nobody moved' (p. 14). We are invited to draw certain conclusions about this kind of community. On the other hand, Western readers have an idea of 'truth' and punctuality that differs from that of the Indians, as is amply shown in the course of the novel. Both this difference in attitude and the need for understanding are suggested in the tolerant, though slightly amused commentary. Often innocent-looking little touches have this kind of effect, as when we are told that Aziz abandoned his bicycle which 'fell before a servant could catch it . . .' (p. 12), or that he, and later another guest, 'drifted' away just when dinner was being served (p. 17). Like his characters, the author is sensitive to mood.

However, he never gives up his detachment entirely, and he never leaves his Western background. At times he withdraws from his characters completely, to make a general comment: 'He [Aziz], too, generalized from his disappointments – it is difficult for members of a subject race to do otherwise' (p. 15). The same may happen at emotionally charged moments, as when Aziz recites old poetry. Then the light tone is dropped and the 'poetic' tone takes over:

India – a hundred Indias – whispered outside beneath the indifferent moon, but for the time India seemed one and their own, and they regained their departed greatness by hearing its departure lamented, they felt young again because reminded that youth must fly (p. 17).

We have already been confronted with the difference between Western and Eastern attitudes to poetry. In the West poetry is a private affair, in the East it is public. The two attitudes show up a basic difference in the emphasis on emotions. In the passage quoted the commentator surrenders up to a point to the mood of the moment. However, suggesting that the Indians are aware of the fleetingness of the moment, he seems to emphasize the element of illusion in their whole way of life: their surrender to the past blinds them to the 'hundred Indias'.

In the following pages we watch Aziz's experience of anticlimax. There is first the rather facetious account of the way Aziz's bicycle is wheeled over a tin-tack (p. 17) and the furious ride through the bazaar. When the bicycle punctures, Aziz grandly hires a tonga and arrives at the hospital in state. However, inside 'the civil lines' he becomes uncertain of himself. At the Civil Surgeon's house he experiences the condescension with which the Anglo-Indians treat even well educated Indians. The facetious commentary is toned down. We are merely shown an aspect of the existing interracial relationship and the way the young doctor responds emotionally.

The chapter concludes with the meeting between Aziz and Mrs. Moore in the mosque. Once they have started to talk there is little authorial commentary. Aziz is again shown to respond impulsively, moving quickly from mood to mood. In a way that is puzzling to a Westerner, he expresses what the moment forces up to the surface of his mind. 'Truth' and 'sincerity' are entirely relative, matters of emotional intensity. We are simply told that Mrs. Moore listened. The way the two respond to each other is well brought out in the following passage:

She listened.
He was excited partly by his wrongs, but much more by the knowledge that someone sympathized with them. It was this that led him to repeat, exaggerate, contradict. ... The flame that not even beauty can nourish was springing up, and though his words were querulous his heart began to glow secretly. Presently it burst into speech.

'You understand me, you know what others feel. . . .'
Rather surprised, she replied: 'I don't think I understand people very well. I only know whether I like or dislike them.'
'Then you are an Oriental' (p. 24).

The authorial comment gives us sufficient insight into Aziz's temperament and situation to understand the implications of the following dialogue. Real communication and understanding between people are only possible on the emotional, intuitive level. Aziz and Mrs. Moore seem to experience the kind of friendship that is only a theoretical possibility at the beginning of the chapter. At the same time his conversation with Mrs. Moore reveals the way Aziz puzzles other people. One is made to wonder whether real intimacy is possible even in their friendship.

The casual words at the end of the chapter appear as a kind of anti-climax after the emotional heights in the mosque:

As he strolled downhill beneath the lovely moon, and again saw the lovely mosque, he seemed to own the land as much as anyone owned it. What did it matter if a few flabby Hindus had preceded him there, and a few chilly English succeeded? (p. 24).

The narrator is acting as Aziz's mouthpiece. But at the same time there is a suggestion that no one owns or can dominate India, because India is not one. The final challenge appears as boyish boasting, while 'Hindu' and 'English' also indicate the other elements in the pattern out of which the human conflicts in the novel arise.

In Chapter 3 we are present at the Anglo-Indian club. The newcomers, Mrs. Moore and Adela Quested, differ from the residents in wishing to see India and meet Indians. Adela, in particular, is very keen on seeing 'the real India' – a request which starts off a scene in which Indians and the possibility of meeting them are discussed. In a way it parallels the one in the previous chapter in which the possibility of interracial friendship is discussed. Adela's fiancé, Ronny Heaslop, the City Magistrate, finds her wish comic, and puts the problem to Fielding, the headmaster of Government College:

'Fielding! how's one to see the real India?'
'Try seeing Indians' . . .
'As if one could avoid seeing them,' sighed Mrs. Leslie.
'I've avoided,' said Miss Quested. 'Excepting my own servant, I've scarcely spoken to an Indian since landing.'
'Oh, lucky you.'
'But I want to see them.'
She became the centre of an amused group of ladies. One said, 'Wanting to see Indians! How new that sounds!' Another, 'Natives! why, fancy!' A third, more serious, said, 'Let me explain. Natives don't respect one any the more after meeting one, you see' (p. 27).

This is one of the 'admirable scenes of social comedy'[12] in which Forster exposes the British rulers of India. The scene shows up the shallowness and snobbery of the speakers, and their tendency to label Indians as a different species. Further, we are shown the wall of racial prejudice a newcomer is up against. In the previous chapter we were shown the Indians moving with puzzling abruptness from mood to mood, in a manner that may baffle the reader and make him sceptical of future communication between the races. Now we move from preconceived notion to preconceived notion, and despair of even rudimentary understanding.

One of the ladies is of the opinion that ' ". . . the kindest thing one can do to a native is to let him die" '. Ironically, the speaker is the wife of the chief doctor of the area. Another lady informs Mrs. Moore that she is against missionaries because their activities might open heaven to Indians, and there she might not be able to avoid them. Seen against such a background the Collector's proposal to arrange a 'Bridge Party' has very bleak prospects of success. The statement in which he announces his decision deepens our scepticism:

'Do you really want to meet the Aryan Brother, Miss Quested? That can be easily fixed up. I didn't realize he'd amuse you. . . . You can practically see any type you like. Take your choice. I know the Government people and the landowners, Heaslop here can get hold of the barrister crew, while if you want to specialize on education, we can come down on Fielding' (p. 28).

We note the facile cliché – 'Aryan Brother' – which does not mean anything, the way the expert organizer (or giver-of-orders) has of ruling out any difficulties, the hint that Miss Quested's wish to see the 'real India' is merely a tourist's whim. The whole passage oozes officialdom. It is as if the occasion is a state visit. This is exactly the Collector's intention: any meeting between the races should be confined to the official, formal level. He simply denies the possibility of any other meeting place, as when Adela objects that she wishes to meet the Indians whom they 'come across socially – as . . . friends' (p. 28). The Collector curtly answers, ' "Well, we don't come across them socially . . . [t]hey're full of all the virtues, but we don't, and it's now eleven-thirty, and too late to go into the reasons" ' (p. 28). No wonder the 'Bridge Party' turns out to be a failure, what Frederick C. Crews characterizes as an 'embarrassing image of apartheid.'[13]

As in the Indian scenes in Chapter 2, the author tends to interrupt the dialogue to characterize, comment, or paraphrase, and, in addition, he is of course the narrating voice. But while he is a sympathetic, though amused observer of the Indian world, he is first and foremost the satirist when the Anglo-Indians are on the stage. They are exposed through what they say and do. Certain features are emphasized, comment is provided that is critical as well as informative. We are told that during the performance of 'Cousin Kate', the '[w]indows were bar-red, lest the servants should see their memsahibs acting, and the heat was consequently immense' (p. 25). We are given further examples of the importance attached to small details or phrases. Thus 'pleasant' is used about voices that may utter dull or unpleasant opinions, the kind of cliché that, as we have seen, abounds in their conversation.

The resulting undertone of irony is perceived in the initial 'portrait' of Ronny, the summary of the Collector's praise of him:

... then he turned to Ronny's other merits, and in quiet, decisive tones said much that was flattering. It wasn't that the young man was particularly good at the games or the lingo, or that he had much notion of the Law, but - apparently a large but - Ronny was dignified (p. 26).

Mrs. Moore is surprised to hear this, and Miss Quested 'tried . . . to discuss this point [Ronny's dignity] with Mr. Turton, but he silenced her . . . "The long and the short of it is Heaslop's a sahib; he's the type we want, he's one of us . . ." ' (p. 26).

In the following chapters Ronny shows how true this is. He emerges as a decent, but narrow-minded young man. He is the one who most frequently repeats the opinions he has been taught. Ronny conforms. The passage quoted indicates how badly equipped he actually is from a professional point of view. Later on we see how his public school training limits his possibilities of understanding the race he is meant to serve (see e.g. p. 79).

A certain effort is made to present a fair picture of the ruling com-munity. The Anglo-Indians are hard-working, fair-minded, at least ac-cording to their own lights, and sincerely believe that they are in India to do a useful job, which no one else can do better. But the amused detachment in the Indian scene is replaced by ironical detachment, with a strong admixture of the satirical. A good example may be found in the account of the playing of the National Anthem at the end of the performance of 'Cousin Kate':

Conversation and billiards stopped, faces stiffened. It was the Anthem of the Army of Occupation. It reminded every member of the club that he or she was British and in exile. It produced a little sentiment and a useful accession of will-power. The meagre tune, the curt series of demands on Jehovah, fused into a prayer un-known in England, and though they perceived neither Royalty nor Deity they did perceive something, they were strengthened to resist another day. Then they poured out, offering one another drinks (pp. 26-7).

Satire like this is a bit heavy-handed. A streak of caricature is made to attach to the Anglo-Indians from the outset. The final line, a sure touch of social comedy, places the characters in a realistically conceived con-text of superficial social routine. The battle imagery, culminating in 'resist another day', deepens the feeling that friendly communication with the Indians is unthinkable. It would, in fact, almost amount to desertion.

Such a feeling comes to the fore in a conversation between Ronny and Mrs. Moore later in the chapter. Discovering that she has met an Indian in the mosque, he automatically starts questioning her in order to find out information that can be passed on. Mrs. Moore's argument that her conversation with Aziz was private, is given a rehearsed answer, ' "Nothing's private in India" ' (p. 33). It is with the greatest difficulty that she persuades him not to let the authorities know what Aziz had said.

Authorial scepticism is invested in the two newcomers. Mrs. Moore's intuitive approach to her surroundings makes her refuse to conform with official India. Characteristically, we are shown how she sees through Ronny's phrases (p. 34). The implication is that he has not been taught to label and compartmentalize people. He, and the rest of the Anglo-Indians, use their set phrases as means of controlling the chaotic reality of India, in the manner of their roads 'at right angles'. But both Adela and Mrs. Moore make it clear that they wish to penetrate behind this artificial front. Ronny answers Adela's logical queries in a cliché-like manner: ' "It's different, it's different; you don't understand." ' She cannot be put off with that sort of answer: ' "I know I don't, and I want to. What is the difference please?" ' (p. 32). Ronny, like the rest of his community, wishes to ward off questions. He tells his mother he does not wish Adela ' "to be worried . . . she'll begin wondering whether we treat the natives properly, and all that sort of nonsense." ' Mrs. Moore replies, ' "But she came out to be worried – that's exactly why she's here" ' (p. 34).

Thus we see that even on the family level communication is difficult because the parties concerned approach the problem from opposite angles. By implication communication on a large scale seems an impossibility. Mrs. Moore probably realizes something of this when she reflects how false Ronny's 'summary' of Aziz is – however plausible it seems. Aziz's behaviour in the mosque had veered in many directions.

The doctor had begun by bullying her, had said Mrs. Callendar was nice, and then – finding the ground safe – had changed; he had alternately whined over his grievances and patronized her, had run a dozen ways in a single sentence, had been unreliable, inquisitive, vain. Yes, it was all true, but how false as a summary of the man; the essential life of him had been slain (pp. 34-5).

The Ronny approach cannot bridge the gap between the two races, only intuition can.

The chapter ends, however, on a note of qualification. Even Mrs. Moore's ability to establish perfect communication is questioned. Moving from the human scene to the non-human Indian setting she is con-

81

fronted with a little wasp. She discovers how different it is from English wasps. We are then told that the wasp, like other Indian animals, has no 'sense of interior. Bats, rats, birds, insects will as soon nest inside a house as out . . .' The perspective gradually widens to include the whole jungle, 'which alternately produces trees, houses, trees.' The jungle knows no barriers; it is the chaos that surrounds – and threatens – any human effort at labelling or establishing links. Mrs. Moore utters two words – but they are highly significant: ' "Pretty dear" ' (p. 35), a common, almost meaningless phrase of ordinary English social intercourse. In the context it seems utterly out of place, suggesting perhaps that even Mrs. Moore's ability to form intuitive links is limited.[14] The wasp does not awake, 'but her voice floated out, to swell the night's uneasiness' (p. 35). The 'poetic tone' has taken over; the social comedy has receded into the background. The 'night's uneasiness' is beyond society, Indian as well as Anglo-Indian; but it is clear that Mrs. Moore perceives it. The words are those of the omniscient author who reveals his superior insight. Symbols and lofty style are the ways in which he can communicate with the riddle of existence.

At the same time the limits of human awareness are defined. By continually linking his own 'voice' with the voices of his characters, and by varying the distance between himself and them, he gives the effect of continual confrontations, which approach people to each other, or bring them into closer contact with their surroundings, where, however, they find walls and barriers at the very moment of communication. Similarly, the way the setting is seen as arch beyond arch, or circle within circle, indicates a search for the 'core', i.e. truth, and a fear that there might not be any.

The Indians and the Anglo-Indians are shown to have diametrically opposed attitudes to reality. For the Indians 'facts' are of inferior value. Tact and courtesy are more important than factual truth. 'Naming', the belief that lexical meaning is the key to a problem, is alien to the Oriental mind, to whom understanding means intuitive knowledge. The heart takes precedence over the intellect and its demands for accuracy and punctuality. The Anglo-Indians, on the other hand, are forever labelling and organizing their surroundings and cling to their etiquette, their formulas and their set procedures.

By using different 'tones' when he deals with the two communities, the author shows where his sympathy lies. He also reveals more clearly why any effort at furthering friendship between the two races breaks down. The satirical approach to the Anglo-Indians brings out their shortcomings. Their attitudes and roles are shown to be petrified, making them utterly unapproachable. But they are also shown to be, basically, unsure of themselves. In labelling and categorizing, they resort to their formulas rather than coming to grips with each problem as it arises.

When, therefore, they find themselves in a mutiny situation, they are not only brought together, displaying their customary courage and determination, but they also reveal symptoms of hysteria. It is as if they have been repressing something that is now forcing its way to the surface. In addition, they are shown to be lacking in the quality which Aziz – and the author – regard as basic in all human intercourse: 'kindness' (p. 114). The fact that cold '[j]ustice' (p. 253) is the fundamental principle of the British Empire, is, according to Fielding, the reason why it 'rests on sand' (p. 253). On the other hand, Aziz's insistence on kindness appears to 'arise from a dream' (p. 114), which at least suggests that the thought, like the speaker's moods, is evanescent.

J. B. Beer sees the influence of idealist philosophy in the 'strong dialectical element beneath the plot of Forster's novels . . .'[15] The whole plot of A Passage to India is geared to the conflict between hostile groups which a few individuals try to resolve. Behind the plot is the yearning for ideal friendship between the races, coupled with scepticism, and countered by animosity. The affirmative and the negative are the real combatants in the conflict, which peters out in the intractable Indian setting. Beer feels that 'the plot which promises so much fizzles out in a negation.'[16] At their parting Aziz refers to the distant future when he and Fielding 'shall be friends'. Fielding asks, ' "Why can't we be friends now? . . . It's what I want. It's what you want." ' (p. 317).

Then the poetic voice takes over, summing up the various elements of the Indian landscape, and arranging them in a widening panorama:

But the horses didn't want it – they swerved apart; the earth didn't want it, sending up rocks through which riders must pass single file; the temples, the tank, the jail, the palace, the birds, the carrion, the Guest House, that came into view as they issued from the gap and saw Mau beneath: they didn't want it, they said in their hundred voices: 'No, not yet,' and the sky said, 'No, not there.' (p. 317).

It is difficult not to see the concluding passage as evidence of scepticism: the reconciliation between the two friends may prove to be spurious, at least if they are seen as representatives of hostile races. Their friendship seems to be against nature. On the other hand, when related to the values which have been established in the novel, and which have just been assembled in a complete system in the account of the Hindu festival, the final passage may be seen as the final juxtaposition of the negative and affirmative forces which control existence. The negation which fills the passage balances its opposite. The 'hundred voices' reflect number as well as dissension. Characteristically, 'not yet' – time – is balanced by 'not there' – space. The sky is again the main 'overarching', unifying element in the novel, but it is also infinite. Returning to Beer's reference to idealistic philosophy, we may feel that the ending is a final reflection of the futile endeavour to arrive at the ideal – the 'real' India which human effort has always striven to unearth.

Gertrude M. White is also struck by 'the dialectical pattern' of the novel.[17] She sees the book, symbolized by its tripartite structure, as a movement from thesis ('Mosque'), through antithesis ('Caves'), to synthesis ('Temple'). The theme of the 'Temple' section is 'universality', and the 'prophetic vision' it contains envisions 'reconciliation on the human level, the cancelling of the effects of the Marabar'. She interprets the meeting between Aziz and Fielding as '[r]econcilation, not real union', because the latter 'is not possible on earth ...' This is for her the meaning of 'No, not yet' and 'No, not there'.[18]

Synthesis is, then, a reconciliation of apparently warring opposites, like good and evil, the negative and affirmative.[19] The way contrasting characters and views are brought into collision may have a similar inclusive effect. Throughout the novel there are references to horses and riders, as when Aziz and the subaltern play polo on the lawn, and temporary reconciliation between the two races has apparently been achieved. The 'horse and rider' image at the end of the novel stresses the sense of perennial tension between union and separation that darkens the moment of reconciliation.

The various chapters may be approached from the angle of a dialectic pattern. We have seen that Chapter 2 and 3 focus our attention on Indians and Anglo-Indians respectively. In Chapter 5 the two races meet in an abortive attempt at 'synthesis', the official 'Bridge Party'. Here we see the beginning of another development towards 'synthesis', Fielding's party (Chapter 7), which again brings antithetic elements together, although the English group seeks friendship, not opposition. Their temperaments and milieu are, however, forces that contrast them with the Indians, and the movement towards reconciliation is therefore real. 'Synthesis' is, however, again temporary.

The next attempt is Aziz's expedition to the caves. Again, although we are aware of the gulf between the races, we feel that a meeting is possible. However, the effort at reconciliation again breaks down, and the result is open hostility between the races. Fielding, on the other hand, breaks with his own people and joins the Indians. Because he is tolerant and determined to break down the barriers between himself and the Indians, 'synthesis' would this time appear to be possible. But again the effort fails, apparently for the same reason as before: however close Aziz and Fielding become, they still speak different languages, the outcome of apparently irreconcilable cultural and temperamental backgrounds.

The synthesis which the 'Temple' section represents, includes the whole of the universe.[20] It almost ignores Aziz and Fielding, both exiles in the Hindu community. The renewed friendship is nevertheless in the spirit of the general atmosphere of joy and release of tension.

The dialectical structural pattern has its textural counterpart. There is a tendency throughout the novel to arrange authorial commentary in an argumentative pattern. The following analysis of Mrs. Moore's reaction to her son's concern about other people's opinions affords an example: She

> thought him rather absurd. Accustomed to the privacy of London, she could not realize that India, seemingly so mysterious, contains none, and that consequently the conventions have greater force (pp. 48–9).

Mrs. Moore's feeling is explained in an argumentative way, as if the 'speaker' is moving from the known 'fact' – London – to the unknown – India – and finally drawing his conclusion: 'consequently . . .'

The language of reason is, however, combined with the sort of insight that reveals the character's central problem, here the baffling nature of India, where everything is on such an enormous scale, and yet is still public. In addition the statement quoted has an elusive quality which often characterizes authorial commentary in this novel. The characters are frequently shown to be bewildered. They are unable to grasp and formulate their situation, being up against forces beyond their comprehension. The argumentative method which may clarify the characters' thoughts and feelings to the reader, is often combined with a technique of achieving insight which may be termed reverberative. The reader is made to feel that he moves in circles away from the individual towards the universal, as in the following quotation, which concerns Aziz's puzzled discovery that he cannot remember his dead wife, despite her photograph:

> She had eluded him thus, ever since they had carried her to her tomb. He had known that she would pass from his hands and eyes, but had thought she could live in his mind, not realizing that the very fact that we have loved the dead increases their unreality, and that the more passionately we invoke them the further they recede (p. 56).

The beginning of this passage is a kind of interior monologue, in which Aziz argues with himself in order to clarify his puzzling situation. But in the second half of the passage we are shown his incomplete knowledge. The receding movement links his experience with that of mankind in general. Only the implied author has sufficient insight to see his dilemma as part of the universal elusiveness that surrounds human existence.

The method may be used to inculcate the moral values that offer the only hope of reconciliation between the races. After the court scene in which Adela retracts her accusations against Aziz, she is given shelter in Fielding's residence. Hamidullah, Aziz's friend and lawyer, comes to see the headmaster, and shows his complete lack of sympathy and understanding for the girl and what she has done. At first the argumentative method is used:

> For Miss Quested had not appealed to Hamidullah. If she had shown emotion in court . . . she would have summoned forth his imagination and generosity . . . But while relieving the Oriental mind, she had chilled it . . . he could scarcely believe she was sincere, and indeed from his standpoint she was not. For her behaviour rested on cold justice and honesty . . . (p. 238).

'If', 'while', 'But', 'For' mark the stages of logical reasoning which makes Hamidullah's behaviour plausible and in a way reasonable. At the same time we have further evidence of the impenetrable barrier between Eastern and Western codes of conduct, because Adela and Hamidullah are equally plausible in their own contexts. But the author does not stop with the girl's 'cold justice and honesty', he goes on to show that she feels '. . . no passion of love for those whom she had wronged' (p. 238), and concludes by bringing home to the reader the moral lesson that is almost as elusive in its rigidity as India itself:

> Truth is not truth in that exacting land unless there go with it kindness and more kindness and kindness again, unless the Word that was with God also is God. And the girl's sacrifice – so creditable according to Western notions – was rightly rejected, because, though it came from her heart, it did not include her heart (p. 238).

The passage emphasizes an aspect of the general elusiveness with which the novel may be said to deal. On the social level we have seen how the characters are conditioned to approach friendship from angles that cannot lead to full understanding because they do not speak a common language. The one person who is close to the Indian way of thinking, Mrs. Moore, is old and weak, and the full impact of India makes her withdraw into her shell and refuse to communicate. Adela's approach is wholly intellectual, and she lacks, besides, the physical and personal qualities that seem necessary in order to break down the barriers between her and the other side. Besides, she is a woman, and the East has not yet rid itself of the conventional barrier between the sexes.

Fielding, who according to David Shusterman is '[t]he real protagonist . . . and certainly the spokesman, if anyone can be said to be that, for the view-point of the author . . .',[21] believes that '[t]he world . . . is a globe of men who are trying to reach one another and can best do so by the help of good will plus culture and intelligence . . .' (p. 62).[22] But this is a creed that is hardly intelligible to his Indian friends. For one thing, it is far too cold and sceptical, touched as it is with pessimism, the 'trying to reach' may well imply a futile attempt. The whole creed breathes elusiveness. Further, the emphasis on intelligence would, to an

Indian like Aziz, seem strange in view of his insistence that feeling is the only true basis for real connection between individuals and races. Fielding's lack of prejudice, his fair-mindedness and good fellowship achieve what the other advocates for friendship between the races do not achieve – more than just rudimentary or transient contact. But his friendship with Aziz and the other Indians does not escape the touch of elusiveness. He and they never quite hit it off, because there are always rocks just under the surface which threaten to wreck the intimacy between them. Fielding is too straightforward and unsentimental. He is an atheist and bluntly says so. When they indulge in pathos and surfeits of emotion, he laughs at them. They, on the other hand, are ready to be offended, quick to be suspicious, and allow themselves to be completely governed by the mood of the moment. At times the Indians seem to be determined to seek a quarrel, and they also seem wilfully to believe in rumours which, if true, they know would destroy their friendship. This appears very clearly in the skirmishes between Aziz and Fielding after the trial – at the height of their friendship.

The elusiveness of friendship is emphasized by Fielding's awareness of its precariousness. The omniscient author tends to step in when it is felt that something has gone wrong, in order to show that the characters, in contrast to him, are at most only vaguely aware of trouble, and can neither express nor explain it. At times they may not even suspect that something is the matter. Examples may be found whenever interracial meetings take place, as during Fielding's party (Chapter 7). In the case of Fielding, however, the author exploits his detachment and intellectual clarity, and allows him more insight than usual. The scepticism inherent in his 'creed' colours any expression of his views. He is flattered by Aziz's friendship and the trust he seems to place in him, for example when Aziz shows him the photo of his dead wife. But Fielding feels sad at his own inability to 'be carried away on waves of emotion' (p. 115). Aware of the impulsive, unpredictable nature of the doctor's temperament, he questions the basic tenet in Aziz's view of life – his insistence on kindness – by wondering if that is 'really all that the queer nation need[s]' (p. 115). In the end he despairs of intimacy – with Aziz or anybody else. The insurmountable obstacle that stands in the way of the sort of experience that real intimacy with Aziz would offer him, is the quality he appreciates most: clarity (p. 115), of which the Mediterranean, above all Venice, is the epitome (pp. 275–6). Confronted with the vast Indian continent, this world of order and harmony seems a flimsy structure, and Fielding does not allow himself to be deluded into a false sense of security. At the moment when an eruption of what he calls 'muddle' is likely to occur because of what happened in the caves, we are told that 'he was not afraid of muddle, but he recognized its existence' (p. 172). Throughout the trouble he is really the one person who keeps a cool head, though he may at dark moments wonder whether 'he was really and truly successful as a human being' (p. 187).

The 'Caves' chapters are the most elusive part of an elusive novel. Wilfred Stone sees '[t]he book's fundamental structure [as] . . . circle after circle echoing out from the caves at the center to the outermost fringes of the cosmos'.[23] Right from the first chapter we have been led to believe in their central importance, as if by going to see them one would arrive at the centre of the universe. We have seen the author's tendency to seek out the elemental in a setting. In the introductory chapter to the 'Caves' section one feels that he is a geologist at work, taking us right back to the beginning of the world. One is reminded of Hardy's customary approach. Forster's sense of system and order may be perceived in the accuracy with which he presents the Indian landscape as he sees it. He likes to imagine that viewed from the moon the contours of India could be laid bare (cf. p. 96).

But as we have seen in the initial chapter, the author's wish to impose order, to name and define, also reflected in the pattern of social intercourse, is countered by his awareness that such definiteness is elusive. This is one reason why he likes the geological or archaelogical approach. The idea of layer behind layer accords with his optimistic belief that the original layer can be unearthed, and his pessimistic fear that such a layer is beyond reach. Thus the 'factual' approach paradoxically reveals both a system and a muddle, and the question of which is the true metaphor for our world is left unanswered. The truth is a mystery, which can only be reached intuitively. The idea of receding layers and circles may be perceived in the structure of society as well as in the setting and system of values. The same basic contrast is expressed in metaphors which describe definite patterns, for example 'arch', and elusiveness, for example '[o]utside the arch there seemed always an arch . . .' (p. 51).

Seen as elements in the realistic setting of the novel, the caves and the Hills demonstrate this duality. Viewed from a distance, from Chandrapore, they appear attractive and even beautiful, but on the spot they prove to be uninteresting and dull because of their monotony and bareness. The whole setting shows a lack of distinction; endless plains surround the Hills, the vegetation is scorched and straggling. The very dimensions of the place detract from it. Like India as a whole, the Hills are beyond mental and emotional reach.

What happened in the caves is 'extraordinary' and puzzling, but it is important to study the 'realistic' basis for the symbolic connotations which seem to dominate the novel at this point. John Colmer stresses the way the author supplies 'clues' which the reader is encouraged to approach in the manner of the detective story.[24] One important realistic factor is the climate. It is almost unbelievable that such an expedition should take place at such a time, but once this has been accepted, it is obvious that the heat must have been an ordeal to the ladies. Much of the inertia and listlessness that they feel may be attributed to the heat. Perhaps both of them had a touch of sunstroke on their way up to the caves.

Adela's and Mrs. Moore's harrowing experiences in the caves are well prepared psychologically. By the time they start they have lost interest in the caves. It is particularly revealing that Adela is no longer enthusiastic about seeing the 'real' India. She is far more wrapped up in her own problems: her impending marriage to Ronny, the discovery that she does not love him, her awareness of serious personal shortcomings. India has come to represent muddle, particularly in her own mind, in contrast to the 'manageable' Lake District where she and Ronny had first met.

In the case of Mrs. Moore it should be noticed how we have from the beginning been told that she is quite an ordinary woman, although in the mosque scene she reveals remarkable intuitive powers. She is old, not very strong, and possibly becoming increasingly senile. Her health has been failing for some time. We are prepared for a crisis by the time the expedition to the caves starts.

It should also be mentioned that Aziz is forced by circumstances to take them to the caves. Once he has invited them, there is no way back, as his guests do not realize that an invitation in India need not be more than a polite gesture. But once he feels obliged to fulfil his promise, he turns the whole affair into a political issue: he wants to show the civil station that an Indian can organize on a large scale. Expectations are pushed to such extravagant heights that disappointment is almost unavoidable. An example of the kind of accident that can wreck Aziz's gigantic enterprise is Godbole's and Fielding's failure to arrive in time due to muddle – the length of Godbole's prayer.

The mysteriousness of what happens in the caves is partly due to the mixture of realistic and symbolic approaches which are contained in Forster's 'geological' method. The fairly sober and factual account of the inmost layer – the inside of the caves – and what happens there focuses our attention on dramatic happenings. Even the echo is rendered as a 'fact'. There is first a survey of the echoes in other caves, followed by the conclusion that the echo Mrs. Moore has heard is not like these:

... it is entirely devoid of distinction. Whatever is said, the same monotonous noise replies, and quivers up and down the walls until it is absorbed into the roof. 'Boum' is the sound as far as the human alphabet can express it, or 'bou-oum', 'ou-boum' ... (p. 145).

We may at this point be reminded of the way anything Indian defies accurate description and naming. From now on it becomes increasingly clear that the caves incident is only to a minor extent concerned with external facts. The subjective experience of the ladies is in the foreground. The objective existence of the caves is a geological phenomenon, but the experience of the echo is a psychological one. The echo is 'terrifying' to Mrs. Moore, not in itself. Gradually we move from the attempt at objectively defining the sound to the effect of the sound on the old lady. Adela is not struck by the echo at the time, but it is the essence of her traumatic experience afterwards.

After the naming of the echo, 'boum', comes the observation that all sounds that are uttered produce 'boum' (p. 145). The account of Mrs. Moore's experience – in the caves and just afterwards – has a firm basis in factual information, such as her sense of claustrophobia (p. 145), and her fatigue as she enters the cave (p. 147). Her general state of health is shown to have predisposed her for the impact of the echo on her. The whole account is conducted by the implied author. This is clearly an occasion when Mrs. Moore cannot see the pattern of her experience, while he, naturally, can. He shows us that her 'hold on life' is undermined, that she has had an emotional experience which amounts to a vision of nothingness: nothing matters, everything merely exists (p. 147). She has, above all, a sense that all her values are shown to be illusory, ' "Pathos, piety, courage – they exist, but are identical, and so is filth. Everything exists, nothing has value" ' (p. 147).

It is, however, clear that the author is not merely concerned with Mrs. Moore's special case, but with the values that are considered basic in human intercourse as a whole. The caves and the echo are related to the riddle of existence. Is the echo evidence of the non-existence of meaning and values, or is it the key to them?[25] One difficulty is inherent in the technique Forster uses in his comment. We have seen how he tends to distance himself from the character concerned to generalize his experience and situation. In the present case the result is that we may wonder if the author's angle distorts the reader's view of what actually happened. How far are the caves the abode of evil or nihilism? It may be useful to consider June Perry Levine's point that the caves are in actual fact morally neutral. It is the echo that is evil, and the echo is 'man-made', purely subjective.[26] In other words, man carries the echo with him into the caves, it is not there beforehand. This is particularly evident in Adela's case. What happens to her and her subsequent echo are definitely rooted in her state of mind prior to her entrance of the caves. Her tactless remarks to Aziz spring out of her sense of personal frustration and failure. In a sense the caves incident represents the moment when she reaches awareness of her inadequacy as a human being, although she cannot express it yet. The moment of perhaps subconscious recognition leads in the first place to hysteria and nervous breakdown.[27]

Another difficulty that confronts us when trying to assess what happened in the caves, is the language used to describe the incidents. We have noticed the factual element in the account of the caves. But, as we have already seen, when setting or universal values are involved the author tends to move away from realistic narrative towards poetic language, the language of symbol and myth. The landscape is throughout the novel personified. It is seen as indifferent, hostile, benevolent (the sky). In the chapter which describes Mrs. Moore's experience in the cave, the area is referred to as alien territory, of which Aziz and his guests make a 'feeble invasion' (p. 147). The echo is an active force which speaks a language, although its meaning is hidden.

The passage which describes the effect of the echo on Mrs. Moore derives part of its force from the image of clashing languages. The language of the echo reduces the intelligible language of social, moral, and religious intercourse to nothing. The symbolic element is deepened by the way the echo is linked with another image, that of the serpent. The power of the echo is first shown in the way '[h]ope, politeness, the blowing of a nose, the squeak of a boot, all produce "boum" ' (p. 145). But then the language of metaphor joins that of ordinary everyday language: 'Even the striking of a match starts a little worm coiling, which is too small to complete a circle, but is eternally watchful' (p. 145). The metaphor stresses the elusiveness of the echo; it is there, but almost inaudible. But the main point is that the author moves from the language of logic and reason to a language which is oracular in function – it does not describe truth, merely reperesents it.

The extensive use of repetition in the novel, not least of words referring to the caves, echoes, circles, arches, accentuates this function of poetic language. Repetition helps to produce the feeling Lionel Trilling has that the book is 'contrived of echoes. . . . a web of reverberation, . . . [which] gives his book a cohesion and intricacy usually only found in music.'[28] But the use of repetition also suffuses the novel with 'non-verbal' meaning. The idea of a meaning which cannot be expressed accurately in words, only alluded to, is characteristic of symbolic language.[29] Forster's use of this kind of language gives him a touch of the prophet,[30] but the way it enables him to convey elusiveness is perhaps even more important. Truth in a way resides in the symbol, but our rational faculty cannot detach it from its abode.

The way symbol – echo – and a language which ranges from the casual to the lofty may play with the butterfly elusiveness is apparent in the account of Mrs. Moore's return journey to England (pp. 204–5). Barbara Hardy suggests that 'Forster is pushing his intransigent material as far as he can in the direction of optimistic hope. The anti-vision is chiefly there . . . so that it shall be powerfully withdrawn, both for Mrs. Moore and for Adela.'[31] This may be too optimistic a view of what happens to Mrs. Moore, in the caves and afterwards. But the old lady on her way back seems at least to regain her energy and wish to 'disentangle the hundred Indias that passed each other in its [Bombay's] streets' (pp. 204–5). However, both 'the hundred Indias' and the 'feet of the horses [that] moved her on' (p. 205) suggest the inevitable countermovement of elusion. The parting 'words' of the hills, ' "So you thought an echo was India; you took the Marabar caves as final" ' (p. 205), suggest that there is hope after all and that the nihilistic echo is the product of her imagination. She is, however, also charged with presumption: who is she to pit her judgment against the universe? The habit of personifying non-human nature may seem whimsical and obtrusive.[32] But it accentuates how, by expanding and contracting the distance between himself and the characters, the author achieves an at times tantalizing effect of elusiveness.

The 'Temple' section seems at first the climax of muddle and formlessness. One may even lose sight of the clear pattern which so far in the novel has both counteracted chaos and accentuated it. The Fielding–Aziz strand in the narrative is one means of imposing a certain coherence. In fact, the account of the final phase of their friendship may be seen as the narrative thread that keeps the rest together. Besides, they are both shown to be exiles, from whose point of view the formless festivity may be watched. It is also important to expose the visitors to the festival and achieve the sort of reconciliation we have considered previously. The author appears to occupy a dual position. On the one hand he writes for a non-Hindu audience; he is himself 'a sceptical though sympathetic Western liberal . . .'[33] There is a touch of the guide book approach in references to facts and details that are of interest to the visitor (se for example Chapter 35, pp. 292 ff.). There is never any pretence of being one of the celebrating crowd. The narrator is always the detached observer who uses his own language to describe a strange phenomenon. On the other hand, however, the author aims at presenting the festival and the Hindu religion in such a way that the description reflects not only the content, but also the form.

To achieve this, the author resorts to a kind of stream-of-consciousness technique when he deals with for example Godbole's song. There is first a passage of authorial analytical and informative commentary:

They sang not even to the God who confronted them, but to a saint; they did not one thing which the non-Hindu would feel dramatically correct; this approaching triumph of India was a muddle (as we call it), a frustration of reason and form (p. 280).

92

Then a paraphrase of Godbole's song is presented, seemingly close to content as well as form of rendering:

Where was the God Himself, in whose honour the congregation had gathered? Indistinguishable in the jumble of His own altar, huddled out of sight amid images of inferior descent, smothered under rose-leaves, overhung by oleographs, outblazed by golden tablets representing the Rajah's ancestors, and entirely obscured, when the wind blew, by the tattered foliage of a banana. Hundreds of electric lights had been lit in His honour (worked by an engine whose thumps destroyed the rhythm of the hymn). Yet His face could not be seen. . . .
   God si Love. Is this the final message of India? (pp. 280–1).

On closer inspection it becomes clear that the author is not really paraphrasing at all. He is trying to convey the spirit and scope of a religion that includes everything, and does not discriminate between the various elements, or emphasize any particular value. The rhetorical question at the end of the quotation is both part of a system which sees question and answer as aspects of the same reality, and authorial reminder of his basic contention that everything is elusive. Throughout the novel we have seen what happens the moment the infinite is alluded to. By means of general statements or questions the author indicates the vagueness and ambiguity of the limits of existence and truth. Another invariable approach is the poetic 'tone'. In the 'Temple' section he tries to bring out the spirit of Hinduism in language that stresses the elemental, the rhythmic beat of form and colour:

As it [the Ark of the Lord] rose from the earth on the shoulders of its bearers, the friendly sun of the monsoons shone forth and flooded the world with colour, so that the yellow tigers painted on the palace walls seemed to spring, and pink and green skeins of cloud to link up the upper sky (p. 301).

However, lurking beneath the display of colour and all-inclusiveness is the sense that even this is a false climax, or, rather, in the language of the novel, the fireworks which are drowned by thunder, are 'the climax, as far as India admits of one' (p. 310). The festival simply peters out, partly drowned by pouring rain, 'the crowds of Hindus began a desultory move back into the town' (p. 310). The singing lingers on, but it is no longer part of a colourful show. The whole emphasis is on disillusionment:

The singing . . . ragged edges of religion . . . unsatisfactory and undramatic tangles . . . 'God is love.' Looking back at the great blur of the last twenty-four hours, no man could say where was the emotional centre of it, any more than he could locate the heart of a cloud (p. 311).

The 'heart of a cloud' is of course the essence of elusiveness. Yet the accumulated meaning of the sky is connection, although the vault it describes is in the remote distance.

The novel ends on the note on which it began – the awareness of separation is for ever joined to the perception of connection. The apparent remoteness of the latter possibility is counteracted by the human yearning for communication – between individuals, societies, with the universe, with God. The final chapter opens with the sentence, 'Friends again, yet aware that they could meet no more . . .' (p. 312). Its formal symmetry is the symmetry of the novel. At the heart of it is an author who through his concern with accent and design presents a balanced, deeply disturbing, yet humane view of the human predicament. The continual pull between hope and despair, the feeling that separateness is the curse of existence, and true relationship a 'shadow of the shadow of a dream' (p. 257) makes one feel that the book is one prolonged attempt to face life squarely in all its bleakness. As Arnold Kettle writes about Forster:

He seems to me a writer of scrupulous intelligence, of tough and abiding insights, who has never been afraid of the big issues or the difficult ones and has scorned to hide his doubts and weaknesses behind a façade of wordiness and self-protective conformity.[34]

The view of the human predicament, of man as trapped in a vast universe, which is, in the last resort, annihilating by its sheer vastness, is one which Hardy and Forster appear to share. Yet the effect of *A Passage to India* is quite different from that of *The Mayor of Casterbridge*. In the latter man is like a vessel stuck in the ice, the design that fate has imposed upon him. In the former the curse is a kind of relativity: nothing is fixed, the design is forever expanding. Yet this very elusiveness is also human: it expresses man's yearning for connection, for penetrating to the utmost – as well as the inmost – circle.

CHAPTER V

Graham Greene, *Brighton Rock*. The Impetus of Authorial Belief: The Novelist as Persuader

George Eliot, Hardy, and E. M. Forster see man in a metaphysical context, but their focus is nevertheless on the human community. *Pamela,* despite its orthodox religious framework, is firmly embedded in human affairs. Greene's Catholic novels are of course also concerned with human affairs, but his religious beliefs give them a particular bias and offer a special challenge to his skill as persuader.

Every creative writer worth our consideration, every writer who can be called in the wide eighteenth century use of the term a poet, is a victim: a man given over to an obsession.[1]

Greene's overwhelming obsession is his deep awareness of the existence of man in a world of sin and despair, the result of man's fall from grace. God may be loving and merciful, but he is also the merciless power that thrust Lucifer into Hell. The fall of man entails an existence on the brink of damnation. In Greene's world the hope of salvation tends to be infinitesimal. 'It is a bleak and seedy and hopeless world which Graham Greene has created as a habitation for both his saints and his sinners.'[2]

The overall impression of 'Greeneland' is claustrophobic: the world it contains is an impenetrable jungle, in which man has irretrievably lost his way. Often one feels that the only choice open to a Greene character is that of trying to stick to a guide of whom he may be aware, but who seems to have abandoned him in a maze in which he is doomed to life-long confinement. Marie-Béatrice Mesnet argues that while Greene 'believes in the universality and inevitability of suffering and sin . . .', he also believes that 'only the grace of God can lift the load', and that we have the freedom 'to respond to the situation we have been placed in'.[3]

The general tone of his novels is, however, so bleak that one often feels that the possibility of choice, of escape from the hell in which man seems to have been placed, is so remote as to be almost theoretical.

According to Allot and Farris,

his [Greene's] main obsessional outlook ... A terror of life, a terror of what experience can do to the individual, a terror of predetermined corruption, is the motive force that drives Greene as a novelist.[4]

95

Greene's approach to the world he writes about in his fiction may resemble that of Christopher Isherwood – Greene's, too, is a camera technique.[5] But the filter he uses suffuses his characters and their setting with a particular colour which provides an angle which the reader is persuaded to accept.

One striking difference between Greene and Isherwood makes the persuasive element in the former's fiction clear. Both adopt the documentary method, that is, like the writers of the naturalist movement they aim at the illusion of exact rendering of the characters and their milieu, however trivial and squalid it may be. But Isherwood does not go beyond the documentary approach of the straightforward reporter. Greene combines the role of the reporting journalist with that of the film photographer, exploiting the cinematic technique with great skill.[6] The following passage from the beginning of *Brighton Rock* illustrates his method, and also shows that Greene is more than just a reporter:

... the new silver paint sparkled on the piers, the cream houses ran away into the west like a pale Victorian water-colour; a race in miniature motors, a band playing, flower gardens in bloom below the front, an aeroplane advertising something for the health in pale vanishing clouds across the sky (p. 5).[7]

The author presents a 'catalogue', a series of 'shots' of Brighton as it presents itself to any holidaymaker. But the catalogue is, on closer inspection, not 'pure'; the passage contains elements that are not documentary. The most striking subjective element is the Victorian water-colour simile. The camera man has superimposed his own private experience of the scene on the 'picture' his film provides. He has not confined himself to the choice of angle and detail. A cluster of associations has been established which the reader, if the approach had been entirely documentary, would have been allowed to discover unaided, at least apparently. There is also a suggestion of something unreal about the scene, perhaps inherent in the perspective: the houses seem to coalesce with the horizon; colour and contour are blurred. The element of elusiveness is reinforced in the image of the 'pale vanishing clouds across the sky' at the end of the quotation.

As the lines quoted form part of the opening passage of the novel, we are as yet unable to relate them to the novel as a whole. But the passage forms a narrower context which further qualifies the catalogue of objective facts. We cannot avoid seeing the bright scene in contrast to the situation of the character to whom we are introduced in the first line, Hale. He is at once established as a victim, an outsider, who clearly does not 'belong to the early summer sun, the cool Whitsun wind off the sea, the holiday crowd' (p. 5). Again the technique may be said to be cinematic. We are given features that any reader may identify as typical of the external scene. Hale, too, is shown on the film, we see 'his inky fingers and his bitten nails . . .' (p. 5). But again a subjective element is added. The author comments as well as shows – Hale's 'manner [is] cynical and nervous' (p. 5) – and he draws conclusions that he wishes the reader to share. The details recorded and the emotions the commentator shows up are used as evidence that Hale does not belong. Not only Hale, but also the holiday crowd is revealed as not belonging to the scene it visits – the Brighton front of 'pale Victorian water-colour' houses.

The crowded trains and 'bewildered multitudes' appear in contrast to the 'fresh and glittering air' (p. 5). The full significance of the latter detail is not yet clear, but there is a hint of a cooped-up existence which a day's outing may relieve. Also, the crowd is 'bewildered'. It is as if the bright air dazzles it. Its reality is so different from that of the Brighton front that the latter seems like a painting of a different period, out of reach, an ideal of the happy life, but even so illusory. The whole passage contains a note of precariousness, of a glittering façade, invaded by the 'multitude', but above all threatened by 'they', the people Hale 'knew . . . meant to murder him' (p. 5). The world of murder and crime, vaguely perceived in the opening lines, is implied in the camera man's running commentary.

Samuel Hynes seems to go too far when he says that Greene's 'camera eye is like the eye of God, seeing all, but withholding judgment.'[8] It would seem more correct to say that Greene combines the art of the camera man with that of the reporting journalist, who, like the traditional novelist, is free to comment and express views on people and circumstances. He exploits the visual approach, but he is always ready to guide his readers. His is not the self-effacing approach of a writer like Henry James. On the contrary, as he has said himself, he 'claims the traditional and essential right of a novelist, to comment to express his views'.[9]

Greene takes advantage of this privilege in a number of ways, which may be categorized under two main headings, the direct and the implicit mode of commenting and passing judgment. The impression that Greene withholds rather than expresses judgment may be due to the apparent lack of direct appeal to the reader in the manner of the Victorian novelist, although this does not mean that there are no direct value statements or criticism. The author tends, however, to avoid statements that reveal his own personal views. He may use a word like 'shabby' about the countryside, but the explicit judgment implied here is based on facts that anybody might have observed and from which they could draw the same conclusion. Besides, 'shabby' is part of a statement which is metaphorical rather than evaluative: '. . . hundreds of feet below the pale-green sea washed into the scarred and shabby side of England' (p. 89).

97

'Shabby' is not merely an adjective which denotes a quality of neglect and a condemnatory attitude. It is linked with the eyes that view the scene – those of Pinkie and Rose, whose first outing together this is. Both are 'shabby' – the children of the Brighton slum. 'Scarred' and 'shabby' personify England, exposed to the ever-battering force of the sea. Somehow the dreariness of the scene underlines the precariousness of the human beings involved, moving as they are on the edge of the cliff. Throughout the outing that Rose and Pinkie take into the country, there is a suggestion that they have reached the end of civilization, which seems to peter out in the thin grass of the Downs. The shabbiness of the unfinished suburb is seen as the last and futile effort at taming the wilderness of the country:

... thorn bushes grew up round the To Let boards; streets ended in obscurity, in a pool of water and in salty grass. It was like the last effort of despairing pioneers to break new country. The country had broken them (p. 231).[10]

The pioneer simile links Brighton, the typical English seaside resort, and the typical English phenomenon of suburban encroachment on the country, with the universal theme of exploration and the spread of civilization into virgin areas. Greene is not concerned with the pioneer effort itself, but with its inevitable frustration and failure. The country in this novel is the area through which civilization has passed: the Great North Road, the 'narrow peninsula of electrified track running to London . . .' (p. 132), the road-houses in the Brighton area. The country beyond is a white spot on the map.

The pioneer simile is not really concerned with external fact at all, but with attitude and feeling. The pioneer breaks away from civilization. His action may indicate revulsion from the society he leaves. He may be an idealist. But he is also the slave of his origin and cannot avoid carrying it with him. All this is implied in the simile, as well as the circumstance that the 'travellers' who experience the scene are as remote from the world of the pioneers as possible. They only share the universal human experience of despair.

The passage quoted demonstrates a favourite way of conveying a sense of judgment or persuasion in *Brighton Rock*. The apparently documentary account of the scene is accompanied by references to geographical features that may not appear very relevant to the world of Brighton. It is fully in keeping with modern metaphorical practice to make sudden and unexpected combinations, as in the pioneer simile. The reference to 'vacant lots' and 'To Let boards' is on the other hand a sure touch of realism, but also evidence of links with the world of T. S. Eliot.

Pinkie we are encouraged to see as the product of the Brighton slum. We see him in a setting of which the sea front, his untidy little room, and the Nelson Place background form the basic elements. But the borders of this little community tend to be extended in a way that is suggested in the following passage:

'I liked Kite,' the Boy said. He stared straight out towards France, an unknown land. At his back beyond the Cosmopolitan, Old Steyne, the Lewes Road, stood the Downs, villages and cattle round the dewponds, another unknown land. This was his territory: the populous foreshore, a few thousand acres of houses . . . It had been Kite's territory . . . when Kite had died in the waiting-room at St. Pancras, it had been as if a father had died, leaving him an inheritance it was his duty never to leave for strange acres (p. 132).

In the first place, this is, again, the language of exploration. It has a flavour of solemnity, as if this were a momentous occasion. We soon discover, however, how limited Pinkie's domain is. The language of exploration is soon replaced by one which suggests narrow confinement. The claustrophobic atmosphere of the passage is partly derived from the way the heroic implications of the language are made to clash with trivial reality. In the latter half of the quotation the explorer is replaced by the rich heir, but the heir's property, which Pinkie is not prepared 'to leave for strange acres', is Brighton's 'few thousand acres of houses', and the title he has inherited is the leadership of a miserable 'mob' of gangsters.

The passage quoted reveals Pinkie's ambition and special type of loyalty, as well as his extremely limited world. At the same time, by exploiting the language of heroic endeavour, the author universalizes this world. We are persuaded to see it as a microcosm, while we are at the same time made aware of the extreme primitiveness of this world and its inhabitants. Pinkie's 'territory' rather than the surrounding country is a white spot on the map, the unknown reality behind the glittering façade of Brighton.

The sense of territory, of areas sharply divided off from each other, of more or less insurmountable boundaries, is a basic element in the assertive pattern of *Brighton Rock*. The setting of the novel emphasizes the idea of opposing territories. The Brighton front, with the long parade, the piers, the hotels, shops and amusements, the holidaymakers' paradise, is confined by the sea at the front and Nelson Place, the slum area, at the back, with the country as the ultimate barrier.

From the beginning there is a suggestion that holiday Brighton is only a surface, a gaudy front, which may momentarily cover up, but which above all sets off contrasting worlds. We have seen how this sense of contrast is evident in the opening passage. It is deepened in the following pages. The Victorian water-colour is followed up by 'a delicate pastiche of a Victorian sunshade . . .' (p. 11), one of the attractions of the elegant hotel, on the terrace of which people are drinking cocktails while Hale is being hunted to death by his murderers. The Audenesque situation is epitomized in the following picture of one of the guests:

... a man like a retired statesman, all silver hair and powdered skin and double old-fashioned eyeglass, let life slip naturally, with dignity, away from him, sitting over a sherry (p. 11).

He inhabits a completely separate world from Hale with 'his seedy suit and his string tie and his striped shirt and his inkstains ...' (p. 13), or Pinkie, wearing '[a] shabby smart suit, the cloth too thin from much wear ...' (p. 7).

It is really amazing that the old gentleman can enjoy such a carefree and secure existence a few moments before Hale is murdered in the underground passage in the immediate vicinity. The phrase 'slip naturally ... away' both throws the lurking violence into relief and suggests that the gentleman has been reduced to a parasite. The attitude we are persuaded to adopt is on the whole critical. The picture of upper-class society is completed by 'a couple of expensive women with bright brass hair and ermine coats and heads close together like parrots, exchanging metallic confidences' (p. 11). Epithets like 'expensive', 'brass', 'metallic', together with the parrot simile release a hostile response in the reader. The precariousness of the upper-class way of life is indicated in the following glimpse of bygone days: 'Three old ladies went driving by in an open horse-drawn carriage: the gentle clatter faded like peace. That was how some people still lived' (p. 11). These people live in the past. Their reality is fake.

In the context of violence and crime the world of the guests at the hotel and the holidaymakers as a whole seems as unreal as a Victorian water-colour. Hale, committed to the Brighton underworld through his complicity in the murder of Kite, finds himself, pursued by Pinkie and his gang, between two 'realities' – the reality of pain, violence, and death, and the reality of holiday Brighton and all it stands for. The two are joined in this 'shot' of Hale on the Brighton front: 'This was real: the two women getting into a taxi, the band playing on the Palace Pier, "tablets" fading in white smoke on the pale pure sky: not red-haired Cubitt waiting by the pillar-box' (p. 12). What he wishes to be real is, however, as blurred and fading as the water-colour, while Cubitt, representing the reality that is soon to overtake him, stands out in clear relief. Seeing Pinkie surrounded by holiday Brighton, the blurred contours are dispelled and Hale has a clear vision of the reality he will soon be unable to dodge:

This was real now: the boy, the razor cut, life going out with the blood in pain: not the deck chairs and the permanent waves, the miniature cars tearing round the curve on the Palace Pier (p. 15).

Hale cannot escape from the world of crime and violence that exists underneath and alongside the surface world of the holidaymakers. It may not be visible to them, but it is there, for the reader a symptom of the shallowness of a society which seems to deny its existence. It is the awareness of such a world that makes the author present the day-trippers as prisoners, shut up in overcrowded trains to escape for a day from the 'cramped streets' where they live:

With immense labour and immense patience they extricated from the long day the grain of pleasure: this sun, this music, the rattle of the miniature cars, the ghost train diving between the grinning skeletons under the Aquarium promenade, the sticks of Brighton rock, the paper sailors' caps (p. 6).

We are provided with a holidaymakers' amusement guide, a realistic account of a typical day in a seaside resort like Brighton. The beginning of the passage establishes the perspective which determines the reader's response.

The repetitive use of 'immense' both stresses the amount of energy which is expended on this one day in the sun, and produces a sense of indulgent sympathy. One is, however, also left with a feeling of futility: after all, the reward is only a 'grain of pleasure'. The whole affair appears childish and ridiculous, but it acquires an overtone of nightmare when connected with the reality which Hale has to face in the middle of the holidaymakers' paradise.

The Brighton that kills Hale is not visible to the holiday crowd, which is only aware of the bright sunshine, the fresh air. The very name of the town seems to indicate the good weather that is so essential to those who have come to seek 'the grain of pleasure'. Throughout the novel there is recurrent mention of 'the bright glittering Brighton air' (p. 81).

It is in such a context that Ida Arnold first makes her appearance, and she always carries with her a flavour of holiday Brighton. The dark Brighton is never visible to her: 'Ida went to the window and looked out, and again she saw only the Brighton she knew . . .' (p. 73). Her view from the window even includes Pinkie, but he only appears as a harmless item in the holiday scene:

. . . two girls in beach pyjamas arm in arm, the buses going to Rottingdean, a man selling papers, a woman with a shopping basket, a boy in a shabby suit, an excursion steamer edging off from the pier . . . (p. 73).

The film camera picks out 'the boy in the shabby suit', and we recognize him, but Ida is profoundly ignorant.

In such a context 'fun' and the good life seem major concerns. The reader, however, with his deeper knowledge, feels that Ida's persistent use of phrases which refer to the holiday type of existence rings hollow.

This effect is reinforced by her fondness for clichés. She responds with her whole body to 'the bright sea' (p. 16), and is, characteristically, fond of Victorian ballads (p. 16), like the water-colour relics of a bygone age. By means of her clichés she stakes her claims in the holiday world. ' "It's a good life" ' (p. 73), she asserts, but her assertion does not include 'the darkness in which the Boy walk[s] . . .' His territory is 'alien to her: she ha[s] no pity for something she [doesn't] understand' (p. 73).

The sense of territory is particularly strong in Pinkie and Rose. It is in fact a distinguishing feature between them and the others. When Ida comes to see Rose, '[i]t was as if she were in a strange country: the typical Englishwoman abroad. She hadn't even got a phrase book' (p. 128). But Ida is, it seems, unaware of this herself. We see her with the narrator's and, to some extent, Rose's and Pinkie's eyes. The boy and the girl are aware of inhabiting common territory, quite apart from the one Pinkie 'rules' over. Their territory is their common background and faith.

From their first meeting their 'common geography' (p. 91) attracts them to each other – Pinkie against his will. Rose is at first hardly aware of her feelings for him, but '[s]he seemed to find something agreeable about him which made her talk, something in common perhaps – youth and shabbiness and a kind of ignorance in the dapper café' (p. 27). The reader is guided to one of the main future links between the two: their sense of apartness, of hostile relations with the world of holiday Brighton, more in particular, with the world of Ida Arnold. Seeing Rose and Ida together, Pinkie is 'aware that she [Rose] belonged to his life, like a room or a chair . . .' (p. 127). There is no question of harmonious relationship, it is simply an intuitive feeling that they complete each other: '*He* knew her thoughts: they beat unregarded in his own nerves' (p. 172). The horrible scene in which he makes a gramophone recording of his hatred instead of his love for her, is in a way conclusive evidence of his sense of shared fate and background. It is the fact that she is the inescapable reminder of Nelson Place, which he has endeavoured to escape from, that makes him curse her (p. 179).

The territory they share is above all their religious faith. Ida enters a strange country when she visits Rose because she has no idea of good and evil, their basic values. Her code of right and wrong is as incomprehensible to Pinkie and Rose: Ida 'was as far from either of them as she was from Hell – or Heaven' (p. 128). Struck by the contrast between Ida and Rose, Pinkie realizes that '[w]hat was most evil in him needed her: it couldn't get along without goodness. . . . She was good . . . and he was damned: they were made for each other' (pp. 127–8).

The common phrase 'made for each other' has an ironical ring considering that Pinkie always keeps Rose at arm's length with his hatred and cynical detachment. But the reader is meant to see the truth of the statement. Nelson Place, their childhood home, is also called Paradise Piece. The meeting between Pinkie and Rose in a way repeats the original fall of man. Critics like Morton Dauwen Zabel and Marie-Béatrice Mesnet discuss Greene's conviction that a result of the fall is '... perfect evil walking the world where perfect good can never walk again ...' [11] During his first walk with Rose, Pinkie seems to adopt a Mephistophelian role. Thunder and rain surround the boy and the innocent girl who is about to be corrupted. As if the 'infernal' weather is not enough to transform the seaside resort into a hell in miniature,[12] we are shown the serpent behind the boy's shabby form: ' "I like you", the Boy said, an unconvincing smile forking his mouth ...' (p. 48).

Zabel sees the task of defining and objectifying evil as 'the ultimate motive of Greene's work'.[13] Declaring that '[g]ood and evil lived in the same country, spoke the same language ...' (p. 128), the implied author asserts the existence of such a country in the face of the values and norms of the Ida Arnold type of world. In a conversation between Pinkie and his lawyer, Prewitt, the latter misquotes Marlowe's *Dr. Faustus*. We may doubt the boy's ability to understand the lawyer's language, but he certainly shares the belief that underlies Mephistopheles's statement, ' "Why, this is Hell, nor are we out of it" ' (p. 212). From the beginning of our acquaintance with Pinkie we are made aware that '[h]e trailed the clouds of his own glory after him: hell lay about him in his infancy' (p. 69).

The quotation illustrates the way Greene clings to the image of the lost Paradise – the idea of childhood as close to the glorious pre-existence which Wordsworth celebrates in the poem of which Greene gives a distorted version. Two views of childhood are confronted, the Romantic idea of childhood innocence and the orthodox Christian insistence on the child's heritage of sin and corruption. Hell is, for Greene as for Pinkie, reality. As in the passages in which country and territory are used to illustrate Pinkie's and Rose's values, so in the case of Hell does the author rely upon the power of metaphorical language to visualize the abstract. It is, however, clear that the aim is not merely one of illustration and analogy. Good and evil have been made flesh and enabled to assert themselves in a world which keeps to the surface, to what is visible. Wayne C. Booth draws attention to the circumstance that although the 'author's voice' does not speak 'directly' in modern fiction, it may reveal itself in a number of ways:

With commentary ruled out, hundreds of devices remain for revealing judgment and molding responses. Patterns of imagery and symbol are as effective in modern fiction as they have always been in poetry in controlling our evaluation of details.[14]

In a novel like *Brighton Rock* metaphor is a major persuasive element.

The territory image expresses the Brighton atmosphere and the particular tensions which shape character and action. But the religious framework of the novel exploits the same metaphor. The same language is used when abstracts like Good and Evil, Right and Wrong occupy the scene as when confrontations take place between the main characters and their followers.

When the landscape of the novel serves as the background for a struggle between moral or religious values, we are in the realm of allegory.[15] The use made of the thriller and of the ingredients of this form of fiction emphasizes the stylized pattern of allegories and moralities. The exploitation of melodramatic contrasts in the manner of Dickens or Gothic fiction has a similar patterning effect. David Lodge demonstrates the way melodrama enables Greene to focus attention on 'extreme circumstances, often arising out of crime, war, revolution, and espionage . . .', and, Lodge goes on to write, 'the narrative aims to excite and engage very basic emotions: horror, compassion, fear, admiration.' [16] This is very evident in *Brighton Rock*. As we have seen, the emphasis is from the outset on crime, murder, fear, retribution, pity. We are confronted with a state of war. Against such a background 'normal' values and activities, like those of the holidaymakers, seem trifling and superficial. Besides, we are forced to choose sides. One of the author's main aims is to persuade us to join the camp of Pinkie and Rose, and view the 'battle' from their side. It is, as Lodge points out, typical of Greene that he manipulates 'the usual melodramatic distribution of sympathy and antipathy. We are led to identify, not with the honest and brave, but with the criminal and cowardly; not with the rich and the beautiful, but with the poor and ugly . . .' [17]

The frequent use of 'battle' imagery illustrates the way Greene guides the reader's response towards the characters involved in the confrontation that fills the novel. Ida as hunter, as the intrepid advocate of justice, is the siamese twin of the typical holidaymaker; she is also the spokesman for enjoyment and pleasure. Because she never manages, or cares to penetrate beneath the surface, one wonders about her efficiency as an investigator. The sincerity of her motives is definitely questioned: the hunt is made to appear as part of the fun of life. There is always a touch of the absurd about her; she is 'something of a caricature'.[18] The battle imagery that is used in connection with her, tends to contain an ironical-satirical undertone: going back to the point where she had parted from Hale, Ida

... stared out over the red and green lights, the heavy traffic of her battlefield, laying her plans, marshalling her cannon fodder, while five yards away Spicer stood too, waiting for an enemy to appear (p. 82).

Spicer is one of Pinkie's gang, and therefore one of Ida's enemies. The battle images convey her clumsiness and fundamental blindness. Her preparations seem pointless as long as she cannot see the enemy.

Eventually she discovers that there may be a clue at Snow's, the restaurant where Hale's card has been found by Rose. Finding the girl unwilling to give information, Ida declares: ' "I'm going to work on that kid every hour of the day until I get something" ' (p. 122). Intrepidity and determination characterize her as a hunter. But the following quotation shows up her complete lack of tactical skill and understanding of the 'enemy's' mentality:

> She rose formidably and moved across the restaurant, like a warship going into action, a warship on the right side in a war to end wars, the signal flags proclaiming that every man would do his duty. Her big breasts, which had never suckled a child of her own, felt a merciless compassion. Rose fled at the sight of her, but Ida moved relentlessly towards the service door (p. 122).

The warship image helps to turn Ida into a caricature. The art of caricature combines a sense of absurdity and ridicule with skill in producing striking similarity. In the present case the idea of a warship in a restaurant is patently absurd, but if it were possible, this is the sort of impact it would have had – crushing, but probably futile. At the same time the battle language enables the author to draw on clichés like 'a war to end wars' and 'that every man would do his duty'. In addition, there are phrases and cliché-like features that have already been established in connection with Ida, for example her promiscuity, her big breasts, her belief in Right. The battle imagery is one of a number of signals which direct the reader's response to this woman. Even features that in a different context might have aroused sympathy or pity, are shown up as symptoms of, for example, her shallowness. The reference to her 'big breasts, which had never suckled a child of her own,' does not soften our response to Ida. On the contrary, the detail reveals her lack of deeper human feelings. There is no instinctive contact between the huge, motherly Ida and the fragile girl. Hers is 'a merciless compassion' – the girl only interests her as a potential witness, or as an object for 'life saving'.

There is a trace of the satirical implications of the passage just discussed in the account of the last meeting between Ida and Rose before the scene in which Rose is 'saved' at the end of the novel. However, this time it is felt that a real battle is being fought, at the heart of the territory in which Ida is a stranger:

> The bony and determined face stared back at her: all the fight there was in the world lay there – warships cleared for action and bombing fleets took flight – between the set eyes and the stubborn mouth. It was like the map of a campaign marked with flags (p. 201).

This time the battle images are related to Rose. The reader's attention is focused on her. It is as if her mental attitude to Ida and the sense of what she stands for have been externalized and drawn on a map. The author appears to use the art of the physiognomists of old, except that he is not concerned with reading Rose's character, but with revealing the gulf that separates the two women. At the same time the universality of the conflict is asserted, '. . . all the fight there was in the world lay there . . .'. This statement leads on to universal images of war. This is not a war to end wars – it is perennial.

Territory and war are so closely linked in *Brighton Rock* – and in the whole of Greene's fiction – that when boundaries occur, they often have military connotations. Pinkie feels 'bounded by [Rose's] goodness' (p. 139). Returning to Nelson Place, he feels he is crossing a boundary, '[e]very step was a retreat' (p. 142). His childhood home has been levelled to the ground as if by an air-raid (p. 143), but '[t]he Salvation Army Citadel mark[s] with its battlements the very border' of the territory where he used to live.

Even the relationship between Pinkie and Rose is rendered in terms of war imagery. This is partly because of the circumstances that brought them together. Marrying Rose is for Pinkie a matter of tactical necessity, the only way in which he can silence her, short of murder (p. 113). Attracted to her as his opposite in a Roman Catholic context, he at times feels a rudimentary tenderness for her. But he usually thinks of her with 'secret revulsion', even as his enemy. On the eve of their marriage we are given this closeup of the 'lovers':

That [Rose's] face said as clearly as words that ideas never changed, the world never moved: it lay there always, the ravaged and disputed territory between the two eternities. They faced each other as it were from opposing territories, but like troops at Christmastime they fraternized (p. 141).

The battle imagery characterizes the true nature of their relationship, which is hidden from Rose. But more important is the way we are made to move from the realistic plot pattern centred round crime and love in a social framework to the allegorical level in which the two lovers symbolize diametrically opposed values and attitudes in the religious pattern of the novel.

War-ravaged scenery is the setting of traditional allegory as well as of the literature of the 1930s. Traditional religious language draws on it. The languages of legend, allegory, and myth share a certain timelessness with metaphorical language of the kind Greene uses here. He draws on the resources of the traditional imagery of suffering, the sum of universal experience, which can hardly fail to awaken an intuitive response in the reader. There is a metaphysical quality in this kind of imagery. Apparently disparate fields of experience are united. Consolo sees the tendency to join opposites, often startling, in his images as evidence of 'the baroque quality of Greene's sensibility. . .'[19] In Greene's use of language and figures of speech Lodge finds evidence of the way in which 'the abstract and the concrete are brought into arresting conjunction . . .'[20] The 'conjunction' itself may be arresting, as in the passage recently quoted, but, again in a manner reminiscent of the Metaphysicals, its persuasive power may be at least as much a matter of style as of sensibility and inventive power. It is as if the writer is exploring language as well as experience and man's relationship to the eternal, at times even making us witness the word – the abstract – made flesh.

The 'ravaged and disputed territory' implies an area which is being defended and attacked. The besieged city is a key metaphor. Brighton, particularly Pinkie's Brighton, is surrounded, the rock its citadel. The thriller plot, with its emphasis on the chase/escape, hunter/hunted chain of situations, focuses the reader's attention on claustrophobic, hopeless confinement within a narrow strip of land. Traversi shows how the hunted characters are 'surrounded by a society which closes remorselessly in upon them. . .',[21] while DeVitis feels that his knowledge of 'the poverty and squalor of the slums' has destroyed Pinkie's innocence.[22] The nature of the surrounding society is, however, only of primary importance in relation to 'the closed theological world in which Greene can trace the interaction of corruption and innocence, salvation and damnation . . .'[23] This closed world surrounds and defends its inhabitants, separating them from 'strangers' like Ida Arnold.

The ravaged territory is the perennial battle ground between good and evil, the soul of man fought over by God and Satan. The confrontation between Ida and the world of Pinkie and Rose suggests that the existence of evil is something only the chosen few can 'see'. Ida is, as we have seen, as blind in this respect as the blind band on the front. Pinkie and Rose, on the other hand, not only believe in good and evil or represent these values, their awareness of them is a kind of seeing. Pinkie appears to perceive the world of good and evil as a concrete entity, separate from the ordinary world, while Rose's awareness is more intuitive.

However, the spiritual world which Pinkie and Rose share is not only of this static, ever-present kind. It is also a presence which has to be discovered. The one who wishes to find it, has to seek it, like a spy from enemy territory. On the other hand, one may also be taken prisoner by this world. Allott and Farris mention how Greene's 'earliest dreams suggested some power prowling outside which had somehow to get in'.[24] The pressure of such a power is strongly felt at the end of *Brighton Rock*,[25] but it is evident in a number of images and phrases right through the novel.

Taken as a whole, the references to the sea have overtones of spiritual pressure. The sea is, as one would expect, a prominent feature in a novel about a sea-side holiday resort. It is an important element in the realistic framework of the novel, contributing to the feeling that the book is an 'utterly authentic evocation of Brighton and what it stands for in British "folk" culture . . .' [26] The sea presents a variety of aspects – calmness, brilliance, darkness, foam, the changing tides. It carries, of course, all the traditional symbolic associations, like the movement of life, or the progress of life towards death and eternity. The pier, the cliff, and the shore suggest time-bound human existence. It is difficult not to be reminded of Matthew Arnold's yearning for the 'Sea of Faith'[27] in 'the slow withdrawing tide' (p. 23), or in the ebbing sea 'scraping the shingle . . .' (p. 148). But although the theme of faith or absence of faith is part of the theological framework of the novel, the sound of the waves grating on the pebbles is above all linked with the Brighton of the holidaymakers.

The waves beating against the pier or the cliff nevertheless contribute strongly to the mounting feeling that there are hidden powers which are continually trying to get into the microcosm of human society, or, above all, that of each individual human being. Significantly, the waves beating, in the end battering against the cliff, provide the music in the background during Pinkie's and Rose's last drive into the 'country' (pp. 228ff.).

Pinkie tends to experience the surrounding world and the influences emanating from it, as something powerful, even violent, which attacks him. The impact of experience appears to be painful, a sort of invasion. Music is a major channel of this mysterious influence, which affects him like pain: '. . . it was like . . . other people's experience battering on the brain' (p. 46). On another occasion we are told that 'the faintest sound of music bit, like an abscess, into his brain . . .' (pp. 108–9). The music seems as elemental as the tide, and as powerful. It represents intense emotional pressure from outside.

The sense of external pressure is stressed by Pinkie's splendid isolation. He appears so shut up in himself that any attempt to get through the barrier with which he has surrounded himself seems futile. This is what happens to Rose when she tries to communicate with him: 'Her words scratched tentatively at the barrier like a bird's claws on the window pane: he could feel her all the time trying to get at him . . .' (p. 175). Personal involvement is seen as threatened invasion: '. . . he had held intimacy back as long as he could at the end of a razor blade' (p. 135). Again the siege image underlines the allegorical appeal: Pinkie holds the fort of evil against the onslaught of goodness.

Evil, and its manifestations, like anger, hatred, venom, appear to have taken up their abode in Pinkie: 'He sat there, anger like a live coal in his belly . . .' (pp. 52–3); 'A passion of cruelty stirred in his belly'

(p. 107). Poison and venom seem to have taken the place of blood in his veins: '. . . a little venom of anger and hatred came out on the Boy's lips . . .' (p. 49); 'The poison twisted in the Boy's veins' (p. 87). All these examples indicate the completeness of his surrender to the powers of darkness: he is the devil incarnate.

While Pinkie never feels more than a flicker of affection for Rose, and only very briefly, he experiences a moment of intense happiness when he hatches his plan of getting rid of Rose by persuading her to commit suicide: 'An insane pride bobbed in his breast: he felt inspired: it was like a love of life returning to the blank heart . . .' (p. 206). 'inspired' suggests both possession of an evil spirit, and the evil opposite of the process of spiritual regeneration.

Pinkie takes Rose into the country for the last time, determined to achieve the triumph of evil over good. But both during the drive and in the interval before the suicide pact is to be consummated, he is aware of a power which with increasing force is trying to break through his barrier of evil. The first symptom is self-pity: '. . . why shouldn't he have had his chance like all the rest, seen his glimpse of Heaven if it was only a crack between the Brighton walls . . .' (p. 230). His splendid isolation is breaking down, and soon he has a 'sense that somewhere, like a beggar outside a shuttered house, tenderness stirred . . .' (p. 233). The emotion is, however, abortive, 'he was bound in a habit of hate' (p. 233).

Allegory takes over completely when we are told that '[t]enderness came up to the very window and looked in' (p. 240). The effect may strike one as stylized and impersonal, but it reinforces the impression that goodness is trying to drive the evil out of Pinkie's heart. The boy senses this power as temptation, which he withstands with all the power his evil is capable of. The more he fights, the greater the pressure:

An enormous emotion beat on him; it was like something trying to get in, the pressure of gigantic wings against the glass. *Dona nobis pacem* (p. 242).

It is clear by now that the power which is 'trying to get in', to the accompaniment of the sea 'battering the cliff' (p. 242), is God. Pinkie is sorely tempted to surrender and receive the peace and mercy of God:

If the glass broke, if the beast – whatever it was – got in, God knows what it would do. He had a sense of a huge havoc – the confession, the penance, and the sacrament . . . (p. 242).

The main distinguishing feature between Rose/Pinkie and the other characters is that their experience of the world is limited, whereas their knowledge of good and evil, Heaven and Hell is profound. This knowledge is part of their personalities, of the very air they breathe. Religious growth would therefore seem to be difficult. The novel nevertheless traces a certain religious development in Pinkie, a growing awareness of the issues involved. The passage just quoted forms the climax of a series of incidents in which Pinkie is faced with a choice between the 'two eternities' – Heaven and Hell. One is the scene in the desolate garage in which Pinkie has sought refuge after having been slashed by Colleoni's gang on the race-course. The experience of pain is important, as Pinkie is normally the inflictor of pain rather than the victim. Hitherto he had taken the possibility of last-minute salvation for granted: 'You could be saved between the stirrup and the ground . . .' (p. 108). His experience of 'pain and fear' (p. 109) makes him feel

a faint nostalgia for the tiny dark confessional box . . . to be made safe from eternal pain. Eternal pain had not meant much to him: now it meant the clash of razor blades infinitely prolonged (p. 110).

Pinkie's experience is a watershed in his life in that it makes him aware of the implications of a spiritual reality he had previously taken for granted. The horror of the race-course incident is that he realizes he has no time for prayer and repentance, without which he cannot be saved. Besides, 'you couldn't break in a moment the habit of thought . . .' (p. 109). Pinkie leaves the garage, 'a young dictator' (p. 110). His spiritual crisis has confronted him with God, but he sticks to evil, and goes straight on to corrupt Rose.

In his relationship with Rose, Pinkie is again given the choice between God and Satan, and again he chooses the latter. His marriage to Rose is null and void from a Catholic point of view. Both of them know they are living in mortal sin. Pinkie's ordeal during the wedding night harks back to the race-course incident. He is struck by the irretrievable nature of his act:

. . . he had a sense that he would never be scared again: running down from the track he had been afraid, afraid of pain and more afraid of damnation – of the sudden and unshriven death. Now it was as if he was damned already and there was nothing more to fear ever again (p. 184).

Pinkie has deliberately chosen damnation, and it is as if by doing so he has rid himself of the fear of Hell. Being in Hell already, the place of eternal suffering has lost its terror.

Despite Pinkie's conviction that he is already damned, we have seen that right up to the last moment the grace of God is extended to him. Salvation 'between the stirrup and the ground' – repeated like a refrain at critical moments – is always a possibility. But so is the vitriol bottle in Pinkie's pocket, a symbol of the evil he for ever carries with him, like his unconquerable pride. The melodramatic ending is in the Gothic tradition: the vitriol is in the end splashed into his own face, and, blinded, he vanishes over the cliff: 'they couldn't even hear a splash' (p. 245).

The hand that seems to withdraw him 'out of any existence' (p. 245) may be interpreted as the hand of God. Has the boy, through his pride and presumption, and inherent bent towards self-destruction, finally used up God's patience by driving blindly into the rain instead of letting the powerful bird in?

As in *The Heart of the Matter*, damnation is not the final word, but the focus on the inscrutable mercy of God at the end cannot eradicate the sense of total annihilation. We have been prepared for such an end since Pinkie first made his appearance. We were then told that Pinkie's 'slatey eyes were touched with the annihilating eternity from which he had come and to which he went' (p. 21). His whole 'career' is summed up in these words. The way he dies is certainly foreshadowed. His vitriol bottle is an eternal reminder of his destructive instinct. When Pinkie had 'bought' Rose from her parents, a 'dim desire for annihilation stretched in him: the vast superiority of vacancy' (p. 146). Nelson Place, which inspires him to such a desire, is, as we have seen, described as devastated by an air raid (p. 143). A striking aspect of Pinkie's cruelty is his wish to annihilate. On his way back to town after his experience on the racetrack, there is this telling incident: 'A moth wounded against one of the lamps crawled across a piece of driftwood and he crushed it out of existence under his chalky shoe' (p. 110).

The parallel with Pinkie is almost too pointed, both in the immediate context of the race course incident and in that of the novel as a whole. Pinkie, too, is wounded, through collision with powers too strong for him. The moth clung to 'a piece of driftwood'. Pinkie's refuge from the gang, the garage, is compared to the beach, which gathers up all sorts of junk, or 'driftwood', symbolizing society and the fight of the individual for survival.

Pinkie crushes the moth partly as a gesture of defiance and hatred. But the moth also symbolizes the situation of man, placed as he is between contrasting eternities. Seen in such a perspective, freedom of choice seems almost meaningless.

Recurrent elements and clusters of images, like those that have been discussed in the foregoing pages, act as signposts for the reader according to which he arranges his responses. The ambiguities that occur inevitably make for complexity in the reader's experience of the novel. The allegorical structure limits the reader's choice of response, but the firm links with the 'real' Brighton counteract the stylizing effect of pure allegory. The gap between the metaphorical and literal may be very narrow. Thus the train journey between London and Brighton is an obvious element in a realistic account of this famous resort. The crowded carriages provide closeups of a way of life and illustrate a social phenomenon. But the crowded train also fits into the moral and theological pattern of the novel.

The train is a recurrent image, conveying an impression of a cooped-up, prison-like existence, essentially aimless and monotonous. More important are the deterministic implications of the train images. Not only are the passengers doomed to be taken from station to station, but the railway tracks are often circular, like the London Underground. Having made up his mind to marry Rose, Pinkie feels that the future has been determined:

> ... he had only to move towards his aim; he could feel his blood pumped from the heart and moving indifferently back along the arteries like trains on the inner circle. Every station was one nearer safety, and then one farther away, until the bend was turned and safety again approached ... (p. 126).

The circle image indicates the futility of Pinkie's efforts to achieve safety, as well as the inevitability of his choice of action.

The most powerful circle image in the whole novel is only evident at the end, when we see Rose moving towards 'the worst horror af all' (p. 250): she is on her way to listen to Pinkie's gramophone record. She is about to be brought back to the point when she thought she had been liberated from her Nelson Place background. Presumably her eyes will be opened, and the horrible discovery of Pinkie's hatred for her will be added to her grief at his death. On the record he tells her to go back where she came from. As she is already back at Snow's and staying with her parents at Nelson Place, one feels that she has been enclosed in a prison of unrelieved despair: hers is 'the horror of the complete circle – to be back at home, back at Snow's ... just as if the Boy had never existed at all' (p. 249). Does the 'worst horror' imply that she, too, will have to accept his non-existence?

The circle image is the last of many pointers to the reader that life is not at all the 'grain of pleasure' which the holidaymakers seek to squeeze out on the Brighton front. It is a valley of tears, with a number of roads marked 'happiness' leading out of it, all turning out to be blind alleys.

Style and point of view are major means of controlling the reader's response. Consolo draws attention to an important aspect of Greene's style, 'the use of a diction alternately plain and rhetorical.'[28] The two lie cheek by jowl in the passage which describes Pinkie's death:

> ... he was at the edge, he was over: they couldn't even hear a splash. It was as if he'd been withdrawn suddenly by a hand out of any existence – past or present, whipped away into zero – nothing (p. 245).

We move from the words of the reporter, with his eyes on the drama of the scene – it is as if we are watching horse racing – to a chatty anticlimax of amazement: 'they couldn't even hear a splash.' From now on a rhetorical flavour is added, interrupted by the colloquial 'whipped away into zero' – from which there is a swift rise to 'nothing' – rhythmically and emphatically standing by itself, with no anticlimax after it. A sense of finality has been achieved.

This command of two widely different styles – the lofty and the colloquial – is combined with a marked ability to make striking formulations, often in the form of aphorisms and proverbs. At the same time a flair for journalese is displayed. The commonest word or phrase may be refurbished and lifted out of the trivial. Several examples have been quoted, like Pinkie's awareness that he and Rose 'were made for each other.' Prewitt's maid is described as 'a girl with grey underground skin . . .' (p. 209). Rose turns her face to Pinkie 'with a blind willingness to be deceived . . .' (p. 93). The holiday crowd walks along 'two by two, with an air of sober and determined gaiety' (p. 6). Ida 'was honest, she was kindly, she belonged to the great middle law-abiding class . . .' (p. 81). Pinkie, on the morning after the wedding, 'had an odd sense of triumph: he had graduated in the last human shame . . .' (p. 184).

These examples, chosen at random, reveal a quality which characterizes Greene's style as a whole: a concern with what may be called the labelling function of language. He tends to provide the reader with a tag or phrase wich characterizes the person or situation. Very often these phrases contain an undertone of judgment. This is particularly clear when Ida appears on the stage. The author is never able to 'keep his fingers off her', consistently loading our judgment against her. A favourite way is to sum her up by means of a cliché, like '. . . it's fun to be alive', or 'It's not natural.' Her favourite phrases are related to her code of right and wrong. As if her own words do not suffice, the author provides a catalogue of words that echo her favourite expressions:

Her large clear eyes . . . told nothing, gave away no secrets. Camaraderie, good nature, cheeriness fell like shutters before a plate-glass window. You could only guess at the goods behind: sound old-fashioned hall-marked goods, justice, an eye for an eye, law and order, capital punishment, a bit of fun now and then, nothing nasty, nothing shady, nothing you'd be ashamed to own, nothing mysterious (p. 78).

By including right and wrong in this catalogue, which focuses the reader's attention on Ida's shallow, hedonistic creed, the author reduces social values which we, the readers, might well consider basic, to empty clichés.

When, on the other hand, Pinkie and Rose command our attention, the satirical method is dropped. But the reader is still under the writer's influence. David Lodge refers to Middleton Murry's 'second category [of style], Style as a technique of exposition', relating it to the classical

113

concern with rhetoric: 'It . . . has an orientation towards discursive and persuasive prose . . .'[29] Pinkie's 'face of starved intensity' is of rhetorical rather than factual interest. The author is as inclined to use clichés in connection with Pinkie as with Ida. But the repeated references to his shabby suit and narrow shoulders aim at making us feel sympathy for Pinkie, while allusions to Ida's dress are coloured by the satirical attitude she always invites. Her shallowness and ignorance are mercilessly exposed, that of the boy or of Rose are meant to appeal to our understanding and compassion. In either case the language of persuasion is used.

Frequently an almost patronizing attitude to Pinkie is adopted. The worldly wisdom and experience of the implied author set off the immaturity and ignorance of the seventeen-year-old. He has not yet had time to reach full consciousness: Pinkie's 'imagination hadn't awoken. That was his strength. He couldn't see through other people's eyes, or feel with their nerves' (p. 46). Neither can Ida, but in her case the author is scathing. One might object that she has reached an age which should have given her insight. But it can still be argued that the reader's response is manipulated by means of language that favours simple and unequivocal responses of like or dislike. In a straight fight between opposing values one would, to quote Ida, have expected 'fair play.' On the other hand, Greene might have retorted that such an argument is of little consequence in a world which is ravaged by the fight between the 'two eternities.' The feeling the reader has of manipulation is, however, a strain on his goodwill and readiness to suspend his 'disbelief'.

The rhetorical aspect of style is particularly pronounced in the imagery of the novel. Richard Hoggart points out that

Greene's similes are almost always short and sharply juxtapose the concrete, actual or temporal with the abstract, subjective or eternal. They can therefore have a genuine and important function in an allegory.[30]

Brighton Rock abounds in examples. Thus we are told that Pinkie 'couldn't experience contrition – the ribs of his body were like steel bands which held him down to eternal unrepentance' (p. 182). The simile is short and precise, and an effect of juxtaposition is certainly achieved. At the same time it is fraught with archetypal and allegorical connotations. Pinkie emerges as a Shelleyan type of weak hero who is made to suffer a Promethean type of punishment for his refusal to admit the grace of God.

Often a simile may strike one as bizarre or artificial, if approached from the angle of realistic narrative. But as a rhetorical devise in an allegorical framework it may be very effective:

She [Rose] watched the woman [Ida] closely: she would never forget that plump, good-natured, ageing face: it stared out at her like an idiot's from the ruins of a bombed home (pp. 199–200).

The main function of this kind of imagery seems to be that of 'bouncing' the reader into accepting what the author says.[31]

Greene is an adept at keeping full control of point of view while lodging it in, or withdrawing it from particular characters.[32] In the course of the novel there are a number of occasions when he allows Pinkie a sort of interior monologue. By the end of the novel the author has almost ceased to interrupt when the boy is assaulted by the overwhelming power of God. The authorial voice is never silent for long, however. There is everywhere evidence of the style we have been considering. The effect aimed at is mainly persuasive and emotive, but the author's appetite for the baroque, the striking phrase is also evident: Pinkie 'laughed again: the horror of the world lay like infection in his throat' (p. 207); '... the woman's laughter was like defeat' (p. 226); '... he [Rose's guardian angel] tempted her to virtue like a sin' (p. 244).

Greene is also fond of extending and elaborating the metaphors he uses. It is above all in such cases that the baroque nature of his imagination becomes apparent: Ida 'stood there like the wall at the end of an alley scrawled with the obscene chalk messages of an enemy' (p. 198). It is hard to see that this simile serves any purpose at all where it stands, but it is in keeping with the overall atmosphere and the kind of language usually adopted towards Ida. It may well be seen mainly as a display of Greene's metaphysical wit. This is also felt in the following account of Pinkie: 'The Boy said not a thing: he had an air of removing his thoughts, like heavy bales, and stacking them inside, turning the key on all the world' (p. 219). The simile is here clearly related to the character's situation, and may therefore be said to serve a 'realistic' purpose. But it is also felt that the author is caught by his own whim and allows his imagination to play with it for its own sake. In both examples we are also reminded of the kind of startling imagery that became fashionable in poetry from the Imagists onwards. The last quotation is reminiscent of the 'What the Thunder Said' section of *The Waste Land*. Pinkie, too, is in a perverse sense setting his lands in order, but the future he envisages is not that of surrender to the influence of the thunder – the life-giving force. The future he envisages is the complete freedom of Lucifer – perhaps before his fall. This vision is part of the towering pride which in the end kills him. The possible allusion to T. S. Eliot's poem cannot, however be said to form part of the persuasive power of Greene's simile, which depends on the one hand on striking formulation, on the other on the universal appeal of the implied action or situation.

Despite the particularity and accuracy of Greene's presentation of the Brighton setting and his compelling treatment of character and action, the various components of the novel are only 'metaphors' for a vision which is concerned with a 'reality' that cannot be reached by the language of plain facts. The whole novel is metaphorical in that it deals with something which is primarily not of this world. The real main characters are abstracts, inaccessible except in metaphorical or allegorical language. The reader therefore has to be won over from the position of a doubting Thomas – by the sheer skill of the author as persuader.

CHAPTER VI

Anthony Burgess, *A Clockwork Orange*. Impact and Form: The Limits of Persuasion

With *A Clockwork Orange* we enter a world which confronts the reader with the limits of persuasion. The novel accentuates problems that have concerned writers since the days of *Pamela*. One is the issue of imitation and autonomy, the question of whether the novel reflects the world to which author and reader belong, or whether it constitutes an exclusive, separate world which must be judged on its own terms. The reader is taken through a world of evil, violence, and suffering, but there is no explicit guide to direct his response to the 'experience' the novel offers him. The first-person approach accentuates this problem, as it does in *Pamela*. The language of the novel differs radically from that of the other novels discussed in this study. However, the basic problem may be said to be the same: how far do language and imagery impose pattern on the chaotic welter of reality and establish meanings and issues that in real life are blurred, or submerged in a mass of irrelevant, often trivial matter?

A Clockwork Orange is a dystopian novel, but less concerned with the details of the society it portrays than its ancestors, for example *Brave New World* and *1984*. The reader is not taken on a guided tour of the sort of community the author envisages, he is merely dumped in it, as in any novel dealing with contemporary life. The affinity between the community which is perceived in the novel and certain aspects of contemporary urban society is indeed one of the most disturbing elements in the novel. On the other hand, one is also made to feel that a timeless problem of for example English society, that of violent, lawless gangs, has been transferred to a future scene and magnified.

A quick glance at the literary ancestry of the novel reveals links with eighteenth-century as well as with Victorian fiction. Its episodic structure recalls the picaresque novel. Frederick R. Karl suggests a link between *A Clockwork Orange* and 'the hermetically enclosed criminal world of John Gay's *Beggar's Opera*, or Brecht and Weill's *Threepenny Opera*.'[1] The hero belongs to the family of young delinquents that includes characters like Jonathan Wild, the Artful Dodger, and Pinkie.

The Artful Dodger rivals Alex in his command of language, and in his ability to realize the comic potentialities in an evil setting. Pinkie is 'his more immediate literary antecedent . . .'[2] The two share a number of features, such as social class, love of music, hatred of filth and shabbiness, ambition towards dictatorial leadership. They are both evil and wholeheartedly bent on cruelty and violence, but Alex lacks Pinkie's aversion to sex, unless one sees the fact that he is only attracted by sex in terms of violence as a symptom of aversion. Both are completely egocentric, lone wolves in a violent world. But Alex is never shown to be confronted with the opposite that Pinkie feels completes him, i.e. goodness, and the values Ida represents, right and wrong, are virtually non-existent. Alex is the devil incarnate, but evil also seems to have infected the whole of the community. We are not confronted with a battle between for example established society and the evil of teenage gangs, a familiar phenomenon in, say, the 1960s. In the world of the novel the police force is almost as cruel and violent as the gangsters, and the 'law-abiding' middle class is reduced to apathy and inertia, watching TV in their monotonous world of flats because the streets are not safe after dark. One is reminded of the state of affairs in Germany in the early thirties, as reflected in Christopher Isherwood's German novels. The 'decent' people in A Clockwork Orange seem to have suffered 'spiritual death.'[3] The capacity for love and affection appears to have withered, and been replaced by universal passivity and indifference. The youth gangs can perpetrate their horrible acts of violence because no one raises a finger to defend or help a fellow human being.

The world that meets the reader in A Clockwork Orange is the sort of nightmare world that one feels Oliver Twist experiences in his workhouse days or in Fagin's gang, and which dogs him long after his fortunes have turned. The vision of such a world springs from awareness of the ultimately evil nature of man and human society, in keeping with the orthodox Christian view.[4] The novel shares one aspect of nightmare with the vision a critic like George Steiner has of the modern world. Alex is a lover of violence and cruelty, and passionately attached to classical music. In the preface to his book Language and Silence, Steiner comments on the fallacy of the old liberal notion that 'culture is a humanizing force . . .' This view is refuted by recent history, which shows that 'a man can read Goethe or Rilke in the evening, . . . he can play Bach and Schubert, and go to his day's work at Auschwitz in the morning.'[5] Burgess reveals his awareness of this 'fact' in his references to Nazi atrocities and by showing that Alex is not evil and a lover of music, but that music releases the same kind of emotional experience as violence. It makes no difference to him whether he listens to music or rapes a girl. Alex enjoys one experience in terms of the other, and uses the same kind of pictorial language to describe them.

118

This is the account he gives of one of his exploits: one of the gang held the woman's arm while Alex

ripped away at this and that and the other ... and real good horrorshow groodies (breasts)* they were that then exhibited their pink glazzies, O my brothers, while I untrussed and got ready for the plunge (p. 22).[6]

When, on the other hand, Alex is listening to his gramophone records, he sees 'such lovely pictures .... there were devotchkas (girls) ripped and creeching against walls and [he] plunging like a shlaga (club) into them ...' (p. 29). His 'pictures' are all tinged with violence. His experience, of music as well as of sex and violence, is orgiastic, as when he rapes two ten-year-olds to the accompaniment of Beethoven's Ninth:

... and then the lovely blissful tune all about Joy being a glorious spark like of heaven, and then I felt the old tigers leap in me and then I leapt on these two young ptitsas (girls) (p. 39).

Music is in the novel the one quality that removes man from the beast or the idea of merely existing. The other youngsters are all propelled to violence and sex by their animal instincts. But music is linked with Alex's capacity for choosing evil and his completely amoral approach to life. Listening to music he experiences God-like freedom:

Music always sort of sharpened me up, O my brothers, and made me feel like old Bog (God) himself, ready to make with the old donner and blitzen and have vecks (men) and ptitsas creeching away in my ... power (pp. 35-6).

Music is therefore the sublimation of evil in Alex – the wings of this modern Lucifer, not a humanizing factor at all.

The conviction of the perennial nature of evil and that it taints everything human is at the heart of the society the novel portrays.[7] At the same time it projects certain contemporary tendencies into what seems quite a near future, like the precarious balance between violence and order, the levelling effect of the welfare state, the threat of technology and centralized planning, the increasing urbanization of society. Characteristically, there is hardly any mention of natural surroundings. The landscape that the Romantics made an integral part of the novel has vanished and has been replaced by the geography of streets, roads, and blocks of flats, and huge institutions like the jail and the hospital. The river has been transformed into an open sewer.

Although these features have been transferred to the future, it is easy to recognize both elements and emotional responses in our own milieu. So far the society described in the novel is a reflection of the time and temper which produced it. One may also deduce from it the author's

* Translations now and later in brackets.

own attitude to contemporary society, although we shall see that however clear one may feel the author's ideological viewpoint is,[8] the circumstance that it is presented through a first-person narrator who is also the main character, is an obscuring factor. Links with contemporary 'reality' help to establish a set of guidelines that provide a didactic angle. The speaker wishes to establish communication with the reader in order to share his experience with him, and, to some extent, involve him.

Involvement on the reader's part depends on the response of recognition which has been discussed here: the world of the novel is different, but not unintelligible to him. Further, involvement depends on a certain realism of presentation. The examples of Alex's response to his surroundings which have been quoted above, suggest a bizarre, extravagant style and mode of experience that characterize the novel as a whole and help to give it its flavour of a vividly seen and recorded nightmare. But alongside this feature is a flair for realistic, factual presentation of the most horrifying incidents, or of circumstances related to them. The account of the clash between two rival gangs is preceded by this piece of sober information:

Now in those days ... the teaming up was mostly by fours or fives, these being like auto-teams, four being a comfy number for an auto, and six being the outside limit for gang-size. Sometimes gangs would gang up so as to make like malenky (little) armies for big night-war, but mostly it was best to roam in these like small numbers (p. 15).

The account of the subsequent violence carries an undertone of excitement that is reflected in a tendency to use colourful language and concatenations of words, particularly verbs. The use of a private language may at first sight enhance the sense of extravagance conveyed by these scenes. But at the heart of such accounts is a tone of realism and precision:

So there we were dratsing (fighting) away in the dark, the old Luna with men on it just coming up ... With my britva (razor) I managed to slit right down the front of one of Billyboy's droog's (friend's) platties (clothes) ... Then in the dratsing this droog of Billyboy's suddenly found himself all opened up like a peapod, with his belly bare and his poor old yarbles (testicles) showing ... (p. 16).

Once the language barrier has been broken through, one is struck by the wealth of factual information, accurately and, above all, objectively presented. The lack of moral involvement is conspicuous. Alex's approach is throughout aesthetic: he sees what he is doing as a kind of skill, or as a source of enjoyment. Experience and object are presented shorn of 'ordinary' emotions of pity or guilt. Hatred, anger, and joy are shown to be inhuman, emotionally neutral qualities, elemental like the experience of hunger and pain. The objective-realistic approach stresses Alex's complete lack of what we mean by humanity.

The realistic element and Alex's aesthetic approach to life are shown in the detailed attention given to clothes, and the concern with pleasant-unpleasant, beautiful-ugly. Alex is for ever recording the kind of clothes he and others are wearing – dress is as much an obsession with him as with Pamela. The catalogue of the various items in his outfit, alongside references to the 'heighth [sic] of fashion' are recurrent features in Alex's narrative. People are categorized according to the clothes they wear, not according to moral qualities. Dirt and shabbiness and bad smell are realistic features in the setting, but they are also obsessional, and the response encouraged is aesthetic: dirt and foul smell are disgusting. Everybody and everything Alex disapproves of, are referred to in language that indicates these qualities. Authority is thus termed 'vonny' (smelly). His Adviser is 'very tired and grahzny ...' (p. 57). Repulsion is, alongside hatred, the dominant emotional response Alex shows to the surrounding world, and the height of his experience of repulsion is achieved in passages which abound in references to the unpleasant. An example is the account of his experience of the prison chapel:

... I could viddy (see) all the plennies (prisoners) ... in their horrible cal-coloured (dirt-coloured) prison platties (clothes), and a sort of filthy von (smell) rose from them, not like real unwashed, not grazzy (soiled), but like a special real stinking von which you only got with the criminal types ... a like dusty, greasy, hopeless sort of von. And I was thinking that perhaps I had this von too ... (pp. 62-3).

The passage adds to the realism of the novel. But its main effect is one of building up a language which in a way codifies the speaker's response to his surroundings. In the course of the novel a scale of aesthetic values is established which entirely replaces that of ordinary moral values. The same effect may be perceived in the use of catalogues of invectives. Such language is further evidence of the way realism and extravagance are juxtaposed. But it is above all an important means of fixing the speaker's code, in which 'starry' (old), 'stinking' or 'vonny', 'grahzny' (dirty) are key 'concepts'. Although stripped of literal meaning, as in ordinary swearing, words like these nevertheless carry some of their original flavour for the speaker.

This is strikingly evident when words that normally indicate acts of violence are also used as clichés about a way of life. Beating and hitting ('tolchocking') are such common activities in the novel that they indicate a mode of communication, rather than a mode of inflicting pain. In the prison, for example, we are told that the warders come in 'to tolchock [Alex] back to [his] vonny cell ...' (p. 77). It is as if 'tolchock' has been used so often in a context that implies beating and pushing along that the two activities become synonymous. On the other hand, the fact that this is possible, is a measure of the extent to which 'normal' standards of decent behaviour have vanished or changed their meaning. There is never any question of kindness in the novel. The question of what it would be like on the stars and the planets receives this answer from Alex: ' "There'll be life like down here most likely, with some getting knifed and others doing the knifing" ' (p. 18).

Against such a background the language of affection, or language which describes what has traditionally been considered decent life, is meaningless and cliché-like. The reference to the author's lady as 'his loving and faithful wife . . .' (p. 21) is horrifying in a context of rape and violence, the only form for 'happiness' we are shown in the novel. The utter meaninglessness of the language of family relationship in the world of *A Clockwork Orange* is shown up in the short dialogue between Alex and his father in the hospital at the end of the novel. His father: ' "That's no way to speak to your mother, son . . . After all, she brought you into the world." '

Alex: ' "Yes . . . And a right grahzny vonny world too" ' (p. 136).

The degree of involvement on the part of the reader is also dependent on the narrative structure of the novel. In *A Clockwork Orange* the picaresque element in the first part ensures a certain initial curiosity based on incident. Within the framework of the town and the surrounding roads Alex and his gang move from adventure to adventure. Even when Alex is on his own, the emphasis is on real and imagined incidents. The deserted landscape and the glimpses of policemen tearing along empty roads deepen the impression of a lawless area, the territory of the knights of evil, who communicate only in the language of violence. After a number of raids on his fellow human beings Alex is caught and sent to prison.

In Part II the focus of interest shifts from adventure to the system which keeps Alex prisoner, and the process by which he is finally cured of his criminality. There is a satirical element in Part I as well; the nature of the sort of community which produces an Alex is shown up. The prison in Part II is a human community on its own. If the whole of the human world is thought of as depraved – and there are hints throughout the novel that this may be the case – then the prison is a true reflection of the world of man, just as the horrible Mexican prison offers a cross-section of human society in *The Power and the Glory*. Greene's version is, however, more convincing. Although the jail scene shows man reduced to utter misery and corruption, Greene differentiates between the types of human being and fate that are found among his prisoners. Burgess, however, offers an unrelieved picture of depravity and criminality.

The main interest in this part of the novel is the cure which is effected in Alex's case. By showing him films full of acts of violence and combining them with responses of sickness induced in Alex by injections, the so-called natural aversion to violence and criminal action is revived.

When he leaves the prison, Alex is incapable of hurting a fly, and would sooner turn the other cheek than retaliate. The mere stirring of an urge towards violence makes him feel violently sick. As music is combined with violence in the films, his former favourite composers fill him with the same aversion.

It is worthy of notice that the treatment does not entail tenderness or any form of emotional therapy. When therefore in Part III Alex finds himself restored to freedom, it soon becomes clear that since he does not regret the evil he has done, there is never any question of a new 'moral' start. He is as amoral as before. On the other hand, it is also clear that he is utterly incapable of surviving in a world which may be cleaner and less lawless than when he left it two years before, but which is as merciless. We are taken on a conducted tour with Alex, in which he is confronted with all the places he used to frequent, even the same people, and with the atrocious incidents in which he has been involved. It is as if the past is being relived, with the difference that Alex is incapable of violence, and the outcome is therefore different. At the end of the novel Alex receives treatment which removes the inhibitions that had been instilled into him. He can enjoy music once more and is, presumably, ready to choose cruelty and violence again. We have come full circle.

The resolution of the plot thus suggests a return to the beginning when Alex was fully able to choose the evil chain of events that dominates Part I. When he is cured of his criminality, much is made of the fact that he is no longer able to choose and is thus turned into a machine.[9] The prison chaplain has grave doubts about the ethical implications of the cure. He argues that the boy ' "ceases to be a wrongdoer. He ceases also to be a creature capable of moral choice" ' (p. 99). The writer (whose wife Alex had raped, and who, ironically, saves Alex when he is utterly down-and-out after his release) argues along similar lines:

'They have turned you into something other than a human being. You have no power of choice any longer. You are committed to socially acceptable acts, a little machine capable only of good. . . . A man who cannot choose ceases to be a man' (p. 122).

This may be taken to be the surface message of the novel. It is a crime to condition man to be good. Like Greene, Burgess seems to insist that extreme evil is better than lukewarmness and passivity. The sort of goodness that man can be conditioned to do will unavoidably lead to mere mechanical reaction. Bergonzi feels the novel raises the question, '. . . in what sense is a man who has been *forced* to be good better than a man who deliberately asserts his humanity by choosing evil?' [10]

However, certain features make it difficult to state the purpose of the novel as unambiguously as that. For one thing, the characters who express the 'message' most succinctly, are presented in a satirical light. They belong to a certain extent to the 'establishment' – at least from Alex's point of view. There is also a generation gap between him and them, deep enough to be almost impassable. Alex is friendly with the chaplain – but for merely practical reasons: he can get something out of him. Otherwise we are made to feel that the chaplain is a rather shabby sort of human being, addicted to cigars and whisky. He is, however, perhaps the only person with human features in the novel, revealing a certain family likeness with Greene's whisky priest. When the authorities seriously start conditioning the criminals, he cannot stand his job in the prison any longer.

The writer is first of all incomprehensible to Alex. When he raids his cottage, the young gangster can make nothing out of the title of the book the man is writing, *A Clockwork Orange*. Obviously Alex has no respect for the writer, who is utterly incapable of defending himself. The two may be said to personify the old opposition between liberalism and aggression. The liberal dilemma when confronted with violence is shown up.[11] Returning after his release, Alex has no qualms about accepting the writer's hospitality, but possibly feels contempt for him because of it. His host is obviously sincere in his view of himself as a knight fighting against a system which seeks to impose 'laws and conditions appropriate to a mechanical creation . . .' (p. 21). There is, however, on all occasions when the writer expresses his views, a suggestion that he is out of touch with reality, living in an ivory tower of beautiful theories. But again there is a human touch about him. When he realizes who Alex is, he forgets about his theories and is only bent on revenge. His case nevertheless demonstrates a crucial problem in the 'liberal' attitude to criminals and the attempt of society to cure them by making them reject violence automatically: the criminal, left alone, may choose to do evil again, and as a raging maniac he may ravage the homes of those who advocate freedom of choice. The circular plot carries a deeply pessimistic undertone. It is as if free choice of evil also leads to a vicious circle, a hell of accumulating horror.

Throughout the novel the suggestion of choice is made by means of the refrain-like, ' "What's it going to be then, eh?" ' In the first chapter of Part I the words at first sound like the fed-up question of a child who does not know what to do. But it soon becomes clear that the games these youngsters play are not children's games, but acts of unbridled violence. The refrain indicates the accelerating speed with which these acts are committed. Each time Alex may be confronted with a choice, but as often as not his course of action is premeditated and deliberate, not the result of a momentary decision.

There is perhaps a clearer suggestion of choice in Chapter one of Part

II. Besides bringing out the dreariness and monotony of the prison routine, the refrain prepares us for the battle between conditioning and free choice which comes to the fore later in Part II. In the first chapter of Part III, which deals with Alex's first day out of prison, the refrain indicates the hopelessness of his situation. The freedom he had envisaged is mere illusion. He can do nothing but walk from place to place, everywhere dogged by the past, but unable to hit back. At the same time his almost allegorical journey reveals how morally stunted he is. He feels sorry for himself and deserted, but there is no trace of stirrings of conscience.

The kind of response the reader is guided to make is important too. The horrible scenes with which he is confronted are bound to repel him, unless he is 'conditioned'. There can be no question of approving or excusing what Alex and his gang are up to. Karl describes Alex as 'a "hooligan", a product of England's creeping socialism . . .' [12] But Alex is not related to a particular milieu and seen as its product, as Pinkie up to a point is. On the contrary, Alex, as Bergonzi points out, 'has chosen evil as a deliberate act of spiritual freedom in a world of sub-human conformists'.[13] There is nothing weak and immature about him, as there is in Pinkie's case. On the other hand, Alex is charming, not least because of his command of language and dark humour.

Such features cannot be said to blind us to the horrors Alex represents, but we are enabled to see the human element in him. Few of the characters in A Clockwork Orange invite sympathy. There are hardly any suggestions that we should feel pity for Alex's victims, except in a very general way. This is probably due to the lack of full-scale characters apart from Alex. There is no one in the novel who can seriously act as a balancing factor. The language of violence and the portrait gallery are stylized to such an extent that we are made to feel that we move in a nightmare, not in the real world.[14] The resulting feeling of unreality is to some extent counteracted by references to the perennial nature of evil and cruelty. But they hardly lift the characters out of the stereotype.

The main complicating element in our response to the 'message' of the novel is the first-person method. Since Alex is the narrator of his own exploits and experiences, there is no explicit alternative viewpoint against which what happens can be measured. Neither can the 'message' of the book be explicitly stated, since the implied author can only operate through Alex. Bergonzi argues that

Burgess uses him [Alex] to illustrate his own quasi-theological conviction that men do extreme evil because they choose to, and enjoy doing it, rather than because they are reluctantly or unconsciously forced to it by social conditioning.[15]

The first part illustrates this enjoyment and may be said to show us

Alex choosing evil. In the rest of the novel the 'quasi-theological conviction' is in the foreground. But every word in the novel is attributed to Alex or has been stored up in his memory. There is no neutral statement of views that can be detached from the hero, whose temperament, imagination, and attitude suffuse every syllable with a colour that removes it from objective reality.

The first-person method lends unity and authenticity to the novel as long as the experiences recorded are those of the speaker. But two major difficulties face the novelist who uses this method. One is the problem of making a character of after all limited experience and understanding, like Alex, represent views and ideas which are beyond his mental or moral capacity. The other problem is defined by Lubbock. Such a method is all very well when we are concerned with a picture of the external theatre of events. 'But', Lubbock writes, 'when the man in the book is expected to make a picture of himself, a searching and elaborate portrait, then the limit of his capacity is touched and passed . . .' [16]

In one way Burgess may be said to have surmounted the difficulty by turning the whole novel into one prolonged piece of stream-of-consciousness. There is very little real dialogue in the novel, only fragments of speech embedded in Alex's own interminable flow of words. The method is retrospective – at first glance the usual 'Bildungsroman' approach. But there is no trace of the confessional element, Alex, as we have seen, being completely amoral and consequently incapable of feeling even rudimentary compunction. The narrator is not a reformed juvenile delinquent, writing about his distant past with a mixture of fascination and regret. The whole point about his story is that it shows him free to start his evil career all over again, if he wishes to. There is a nostalgic element in his account of his early life, but this is due to what happens to him in prison, not to the fact that it is irretrievable.

The total lack of normal emotional equipment enables Alex to reveal his own complete depravity without the embarrassing overtones that burden the criminal-turned-respectable in a certain type of confessional novel. Plausibility is nevertheless a problem. We have only Alex's word for the truth of his account of himself. At times one may be pardoned for suspecting him of exaggerating and bragging. This suspicion is strengthened by the circumstance that Alex does not distinguish between fact and fiction. His experience of bliss and happiness when immersed in violence is, as we have seen, if anything more intense when he is lying on his bed listening to music than when he is actively inflicting pain on his fellow human beings. Also, he moves quickly and easily from dream to reality, one mode of enjoying violence being as real to him as the other. It might also be argued that he revels in the language of violence, the colourful words with which he records his evil exploits and evil thoughts, as much as in the act itself. At times one is made to feel that it is the word made flesh that concerns him, the art with which he enables evil to take up its abode in language.[17]

Because Alex is such a master of words and obviously both intelligent and highly critical of the views and language of other people, it is obviously very difficult to make him a plausible medium for ideas that are only relevant to his situation as abstractions. He shows that he invariably chooses evil when he has a chance. His case demonstrates the effect of a cure, and he tells us about it in his own colourful language as his personal, unique experience. But abstractions – generalized statements of theories – do not fit into his language. The 'quasi-theological' author seems to require this kind of statement, so he resorts to the method often used in the novels of ideas, confronting the inexperienced Alex with experts in a dialogue. The effect is ironical, and is obviously intended to be so. Alex's language is contrasted with 'scientific' language, the language of a bygone period – the age of the 'starry vecks' (old men). It is, from the point of view of the narrator and his generation, out-of-date, queer, and obscure. The reader is made to feel that it is shallow and devoid of feeling and conviction. Inevitably both Alex and the reader question the truth and sincerity of the views the opponents of 'Reclamation Treatment' express. The reader may also feel that the victim is left completely out of account in this world in which egocentricity is carried to absurd lengths. The way the style of the pseudo-philanthropists is made suspect is shown in a passage which also records Alex's reading and comments on *A Clockwork Orange:*

It seemed written in a very bezoomny (mad) like style, full of Ah and Oh and that cal (faeces), but what seemed to come out of it was that all lewdies (people) nowadays were being turned into machines and that they were really – you and me and kiss-my-sharries (buttocks) – more like a natural growth like a fruit. F. Alexander seemed to think that we all like grow on what he called the world-tree in the world-orchard that like Bog or God planted, and we were there because Bog or God had need of us to quench his thirsty love, or some such cal (p. 124).

'quench his thirsty love' sounds like a worn-out sentimental cliché at the best of times, but in the context of Alex's language and hostility it is simply demolished. One wonders if the underlying idea can survive.

It would seem that the ideological aspect of the novel is presented as a symptom of the general de-humanizing process which has turned the community to which Alex belongs into a community of machines. Even the antagonists of the system seem to have been stripped of emotional involvement, their approach being wholly theoretical. A crucial passage as regards ideas is the one in which Alex, the day before his release, confronted with a roomful of experts and dignitaries, exclaims,

'Me, me, me. How about me? Where do I come into all this? Am I like just some animal or dog? ... Am I just to be like a clockwork orange?' (p. 100).

Alex here emerges as a protester against a system of oppression, and as such he may be seen as the author's spokesman. But it is part of the implied vision of this future society that the protest is futile, because it has come too late. Whatever happens to Alex, the emotional climate is the same; people have already been reduced to animals and things, and the authorities think of them as such.

It seems, then, that Alex can only be seen as the author's spokesman in a very general way. He may be taken to be a kind of exemplum, representing the prospect of unbridled violence in a steamrolled welfare state where all human intercourse has broken down. On the other hand, one suspects that he is also in some respects an ideal, the potentially strong, beautiful, intelligent, ruthless leader type, who might, under different circumstances, have turned into an ideal soldier-statesman and reinfused an inert society with health and vigour. Perhaps this is the 'good' alternative that is never chosen?

The total impression of *A Clockwork Orange* is one of a nightmare world, complete and enclosed within its circular form, but close enough to our own reality to leave the reader deeply disturbed.

Language is a major means of establishing Alex's separate world. It is largely private, 'a special kind of slang that incorporates a large number of words of Russian origin ...' [18] It spans the lofty and the low in the English language. Alex and, presumably, his friends, finding it hard to understand the 'scientific' language of the older generation, use the rhythms and vocabulary of Biblical English. There is also a touch of Shakespeare in Alex's style, not least in his fondness for 'catalogues' of words, particularly, as we have seen, of invective. As in the case of Shakespeare, there is also a pronounced tendency to surrender to the sounds of language. Words may be said to affect Alex in a similar way to music. In his protest against the 'system' he uses the phrase 'clockwork orange' without thinking of its meaning; indeed, he is very uncertain about it. The words themselves fascinate him. Even when he is being cured and the films shown him make him feel thoroughly sick, he cannot avoid revelling in the words with which he describes them: the films, we are told, were

all of smecking malchicks (laughing boys) doing the ultra-violent on a young ptitsa (girl) who was creeching away in her red red krovvy (blood), her platties all razressed (ripped) real horrorshow' (p. 88).

The language takes away from the horror of the scene for the reader, here and elsewhere in the book. Above all, the use of strange and unintelligible words about horrors that are in themselves unbearable, makes the reader and, we suspect, the speaker as well, divide their attention between 'reality' and the magic of sound and rhythm that turn it into a sort of sleeping beauty.[19] The enchanted garden of language becomes almost an end in itself. This feeling is deepened when we discover the extensive use that is made of mere repetition of sounds and verbal elements regardless of vocabular meaning. The blood always tends to be referred to as 'red red krovvy', with the result that the brutal fact of blood is gradually lost sight of. One suspects that 'razrezzed' is preferred to 'ripped' because of its repetitive sound pattern. The repetition of 'high' and 'bubble' in the following examples is of no lexical significance: 'And then a top millicent (policeman) came in with like stars on his pletchoes (shoulders) to show he was high high high...' (p. 55); a boy had his wrist slashed, 'and there was too much krovvy (blood) to drink and he went bubble bubble bubble...' (p. 45). The feeling of exuberance and the sense of comedy that counteract the feeling of horror may be traced to the play with words for their own sake. This is particularly evident in the use of words that are made up of rhyming syllables, a feature which a certain type of slang shares with traditional nursery rhymes and nonsense verse: 'I had just ticklewickled his fingers with my britva (razor)...' (p. 44); 'her veiny mottled litso going purplewurple...' (p. 51). At times a sort of rhyming contest seems to be going on: '... I still felt shagged and fagged and fashed and bashed...' (p. 30); 'My dad was like humble mumble chumble' (p. 40).

The systematic use of repetition of various kinds – of sounds and sound patterns, the 'red red krovvy' type of words, phrases, units, with varying regularity in the course of the book – helps to impose a stylized, formal pattern on the experience the novel sets out to portray. It helps to focus the reader's attention on the aesthetic approach which, as we have seen, characterizes Alex. The verbal expression of the experience has been pushed into the foreground. We are invited to surrender to the orchestral magic of his language, the secret of his devilish charm.

A lively sense of rhythm is at the heart of this language. It is felt in its archaisms, the lilting flowing rhythm of the Bible-flavoured style: ' "... let us be on our way, O my brothers" ' (p. 18); ' "Never worry about thine only son and heir, O my father..." ' (p. 41). 'O my brother' and similar phrases are so much part of Alex's idiom that they have almost lost their lexical meaning. They seem to serve mainly rhythmical purposes, such as the 'like' with which he peppers his language. It is of course deeply ironical that brother and other family words should occur so often in the language of a person who is so singularly free from family feeling. But it is the reader who has to make this kind of reflection.

Connecting words like 'and' and 'then' are used in abundance, and help to secure the epic effect that is such an important link between the narrator and the reader. But again rhythm is perhaps even more important. We see this in a tendency to split a statement up into groups of words by means of 'and'. The rhythmic beat of the paragraph requires expansion, not concentration: when raiding a house, Alex is suddenly surrounded by cats: 'I . . . found that like fur and teeth and claws had like fastened themselves round my leg . . .' (p. 52). (The passage also demonstrates the rhythmic usefulness of 'like'.) In one of the prison incidents we are told that the warders 'came along in their shirts and trousers and caps, waving big sticks' (p. 70).

'Then' often denotes the 'now', which is the point from which the narrator plunges into his experience – verbal or 'real' – and to which he returns before his next plunge. The result is a particular type of rhythmical effect which indicates the persistence of a trivial, straightforward time element, measured by 'then', unquenchable by the horror of the moment. Also, it defines the limits within which a world partaking of fantasy as well as 'fact' is confined. The raid on the writer's cottage affords an example, too long to be quoted: the woman is being raped, first by Alex, then by the others in turn. 'Then' interrupts each horrible, wordy installment, briefly and precisely (p. 22). The rhythmic cadence is also achieved by the alternation between long, sweeping sentences and brief, bare statements of 'facts': 'Then there was a change-over . . .', followed by, '. . . Dim and me grabbing the slobbering writer veck who was past struggling really, only just coming out with slack sort of slovos (words) like he was in the land (drugs) in a milk-plus bar . . .' (p. 22).

Drugs and drinking are, as one would expect, important means of escaping from a dull and horrible world in *A Clockwork Orange*. At the height of his glory Alex feels that orgies of violence along deserted streets are superior to the bliss drugs can provide, but the bar where he and his friends can buy milk mixed with drugs is the base from which they make their forays into the surrounding no man's land, so it seems drugs are part of their experience of joy when inflicting pain and suffering on others. But music and, above all, words are Alex's main drugs. He sees in 'pictures' (p. 136), mixtures of dream and reality. He is, perhaps, more sensitive to the way a voice sounds than anything else. Voices and the art of listening are entrances to the only heaven Alex can envisage: in his old room at home, supplied with full stereo equipment, he can listen to Beethoven's Fifth and transfer his sensations into words. Does the title *A Clockwork Orange* also refer to this kind of mechanically produced bliss? Maybe the novel itself represents a fictional world which in the perfection of its structure and language constitutes a 'clockwork orange', completely self-contained and stripped of all humanity.

The reader has been brought up to the limits of persuasion. He moves in the course of the novel from his first intuitive response of repulsion and horror at acts of violence and inhumanity, through awareness of a world in which such features dominate, to a final recognition that pattern – the aesthetics of form – has replaced life, with its emphasis on ethical values.

Conclusion

All the novels discussed in this study reveal their creator's dilemma: fascination with language and form is balanced by the vision of a world which is influenced by moral or religious values. Preoccupation with form makes for an autonomous world – that of the novel as a work of art. As a visionary the novelist looks in two directions – towards the microcosm which he is creating, and towards the world to which he belongs. In novels like *Pamela* and *A Clockwork Orange* the first person method of narration obscures the contours of the resulting dilemma, while the other novels display the agility with which the author may move between the two worlds. They all reveal his exploitation of the omniscient point of view to show up the characters' limited awareness and knowledge. The bleakness of his outlook compared to theirs appears to be the result of his wider horizon. Not only is he their creator, he also draws on the heritage of the 'real' world, good and bad, and it is this heritage that often determines his vision.

While the author's fictitious characters are detached from the world of ordinary mortals, the readers share this world with him. Their judgment, the product of intellect and milieu, is brought to bear upon the world of fiction. The art of persuasion includes the network of devices by which the author exploits the reader's pre-existing framework of responses and entices him to accept the impulse the fictional world releases. Novels like *Pamela, Brighton Rock,* and *A Clockwork Orange* demonstrate the skill with which the reader's stores of clichés and stock responses are manipulated. The author may draw on the resources of language as well as the common tradition of stereotyped roles, situations, or motifs. It is part of the writer's art as well as his dilemma to make this hackneyed material come alive and incorporate it in the 'experience' of the characters in his work. It may of course also be used for satirical purposes, as shown in *A Passage to India* and *Brighton Rock.*

The art of persuasion is also an integral part of the writer's creative imagination. The way he unites the gift of the creator with that of the artificer suggests that he faces in two directions in this respect too: he is on the one hand concerned with the shape and content of his work for its own sake, on the other with its impact upon his readers. In both cases he may unite a vision of chaos and destruction with a yearning for order and clarity. In a novel like *A Passage to India*, a sense of pattern which eludes the rigidity of formal language is balanced by the awareness of an all-embracing chaos.

The inhabitants of the world of fiction may display individual freedom of action. They may appear to be the masters of their own fate, or be able to determine their relationships. The reader is aware, however, that this is an illusion, though it is part of the game that he should be prepared to suppress his scepticism. The characters in a novel are felt to be akin to the inhabitants of the reader's own world. *The Mayor of Casterbridge* demonstrates how a particular character may be made to serve as the authorial norm, thus securing a particular angle of vision. But in all the novels one may perceive a pull in certain characters between their rights as 'individuals' and their functions as representatives. Pamela represents purity and virtue, but the situation in which she finds herself releases personal qualities like courage and endurance, and turns the moral exemplum into a suffering human being. On the other hand, the Anglo-Indian women in *A Passage to India,* or Ida Arnold in *Brighton Rock* never allow the reader to forget their main function: that of persuading him to reject the system to which they belong. *Silas Marner,* however, shows that the persuasive power of the underlying moral fable, reinforced by the recurrence of certain features in the setting, need not dwarf the interest we are invited to take in the characters for their own sake. We are not allowed to forget that although the moral message may be of general validity, it is the special concern of a particular group of characters.

Form and language are in themselves major persuasive elements, providing the trajectory of the reader's response. In the group of novels dealt with here, *A Clockwork Orange* represents the utmost limits to which a writer may go. Burgess highlights a problem which he shares with every other writer. His novel is inspired by a nightmarish vision of the human world, based on moral values. But his vision is enclosed in a work of art which focuses the reader's attention on aesthetic values, being in itself an instance of formal perfection. The reader is persuaded to accept the prospect of a future which is completely amoral, but he must decide for himself whether this view is relevant only within the closed world of the novel. '

It is easy to over-elaborate the art of persuasion. All verbal communication is in the last resort a matter of persuasion. If one distinguishes between 'private' and 'public' use of language and considers the language of fiction to be in the latter category, the question of impact upon a listener or reader becomes even more clearly a general concern, equally characteristic of all forms of discourse.[1]

Yet the art of persuasion has provided a useful and illuminating approach to the six novels which have been studied here. Certain conclusions can be drawn which have general relevance to all fiction. Again one has to move carefully. Because so many of the determining factors in the author–work–reader relationship are of an elusive and undefinable kind which defy exact description, one is easily tempted to resort to truisms or facile generalisations.

A basic factor in the reader's response is a trap of this kind: the set of expectations he brings with him to the act of reading a novel. Some of these can of course be charted by means of sociological investigation. One may also subject the reader to the kind of test to which I. A. Richards subjected his students while he was preparing his *Practical Criticism*. The present work has not tried to chart the reader's response or to trace it in any systematic way. Certain assumptions have been made, and the trap of truism has been avoided by trying to keep as closely as possible to the work as experienced by at least one reader. Indirectly the responses of a great number of student readers have inevitably helped to shape the underlying notion of *the* reader.

The advantage of this rather empirical approach to the problem of the reader's expectations is that one is enabled to watch the way expectations are both exploited and modified in ways that are among the distinguishing prerogatives of the novelist compared to other types of writer. Despite the changing attitudes to reality in the course of the novel's lifetime any reader expects to find certain elements in the novel that he can recognize as real – a circumstance that makes Goldknopf define reality as 'whatever we experience as actually or potentially comprehensible'.[2] Consequently, as he reads the novel, the reader is looking for such comprehensible elements, and there are plenty of them, for example references to or descriptions of settings, people or actions. The first complicating factor, which the reader cannot anticipate, is the principle of selection which is axiomatic in any recording of reality. The features the novelist has put down on paper represent rather than present the reality he is offering the reader. In other words, he offers a version of reality. This fact may be exploited by the novelist, as when Graham Greene in *Brighton Rock* juxtaposes holiday Brighton and the Brighton of the slums, or when E. M. Forster confronts the reader with Indias rather than India and makes a special point of presenting a sequence in which the reader is made to alternate between the Indian and the Anglo-Indian milieus.

There is a persuasive potentiality hidden in the author's skill in applying the principle of selection. His novel may be shaped so as to show the reader that his expectations are wrong or misleading, or that he does not know the truth but will now be able to find it. The reader is often taken from the initial implied assumption that he knows reality to the recognition that what has seemed real to him is not true. In other words, reality has been hidden from him, his initial expectations were wrong.

The books studied in this work show that all aspects of the novelist's craft can be exploited to achieve such an effect. The elements of surprise, complication, and suspense in the narrative pattern of the crime story are in *Brighton Rock* made to serve the purpose of confronting the reader with a hidden spiritual reality. In *The Mayor of Casterbridge* a particular character emerges as observer and judge, thus securing a reliable platform for assessing human society and values.

The treatment of setting is particularly illuminating, and also unique because the novel alone among literary forms exploits to the full the potentialities of landscape and setting. The setting may be presented to the reader in different ways, but three basic modes are very much in evidence in the novels included in this work, and indeed in most novels. One is the assumption that the setting is really there, yet the reader has still to be invited to enter. The opening of *The Mayor of Casterbridge,* which shows us a man, a woman and a child walking along a dusty road, could be seen as the usual way in which the reader is introduced to the setting of the story,[3] although the traveller image may not be so prominent. Another approach is that of the architect or designer: we feel that the novelist does not merely pretend to describe what is there, but also acts as landscape gardener and creates something that was not there before. The design is something he invites the reader to explore or discover, as he does in *Silas Marner, The Mayor of Casterbridge, A Passage to India, Brighton Rock* and a host of other novels. The third mode of presenting setting is the metaphorical one, and this is where both the representational and the persuasive functions of setting are most clear and most exploited in ways that are specific to fiction. In all the novels certain elements in the setting have been selected and given special significance, and the point of reference is the reader rather than the characters in the story. The allegorical element in most of the novels is directed to the reader, and so are a number of specific details that are given symbolic significance, for example the door in *Silas Marner*, the window in *The Mayor of Casterbridge*, the hills and the caves in *A Passage to India*, and a number of features in the landscape of *Brighton Rock*.

Both the impression of design and the selection of significant details reinforce the experience the reader has of being given more than he expects − that he is invited to modify his conception of reality, perhaps recognize that his version of it is an illusion. The novelist is also in this respect a conscious plotter; this is shown most clearly in *A Passage to India* and *Brighton Rock,* but it is also implied in the other novels, most notably in *A Clockwork Orange.*

In the latter novel two sets of expectations the reader may be assumed to bring with him to the reading of the novel are frustrated – those relating to form and those relating to value and conduct. Clearly a number of formal expectations are assumed both by author and reader. There is the basic requirement of a tale of a certain length, of character, and of action. Certain features in the novel are conventional, and certain roles, types, and motifs tend to recur over long periods. The six novels we have examined offer evidence of the amazingly long life some of these features have, presumably because they are closely concerned with what have always been considered essential aspects of the human condition. On the other hand, the very fact that certain conventions have become stereotyped, part of our everyday world as clichés or stock responses, has turned these conventions into a goldmine for the satirical or didactic writer. In fact, because they are so much part of the reader's unconscious expectation, any novelist may exploit them to bring about the experience of novelty and excitement that appears to be a central element in the experience of reading. It can be problematic to assess this element, particularly when one is dealing with a novel like *Pamela,* which after all appeared over two hundred years ago. In such a case it is not all that easy to determine the value of a cliché or a stereotyped role. But *Pamela* is a particularly rewarding case for the study of the manner in which convention is modified or tested in the course of the reading process. Presumably Samuel Richardson as a didactic writer wishes to inculcate the moral tenets that form the basis of the novel, and which the reader, one supposes, is meant to take for granted. These tenets are expressed through certain fixed roles and attitudes, and articulated in an idiom that abounds in clichés and memorable sayings. But the experiences that are the subject of *Pamela* are unique and in some measure liberated from their conventional context. It is this sense of crisis and uniqueness that makes the reader experience a sense of novelty and change: even clichés are given a new and serious meaning. In the process we are also brought close to the heroine's heart, a cliché that has been refurbished by the reality of personal experience.

This sort of confrontation between convention and crisis – the unique – is continually exploited by novelists. The power to arrest the reader's attention and in so doing make him aware of the true nature of reality is perhaps one of the criteria of the novel as an art. The novels in this study abound in examples of the way the conventional, related to the novel form as well as to conduct and idiom, is modified or exposed by some crisis situation in which certain characters find themselves, or by the moment of illumination the author enables the reader to experience. This type of experience is in the foreground in *Silas Marner, The Mayor of Casterbridge,* and *A Passage to India.* In *Brighton Rock* the confrontation between the conventional and the unique or 'real' is pointed out by the authorial narrator/commentator. In *A Clockwork Orange* a confrontation is implied, partly through certain conventional narrative elements, for example the picaresque mode, or the expectations contained in the traditional tale, partly through the dramatic confrontation, through dialogue and first-person narrative, between old and new modes of speaking.

A Clockwork Orange attaches particular importance to the reader's expectations as to value and behaviour. The ambiguity of the novel is largely due to the fact that while 'normal' standards of behaviour are assumed from the start, and it is perhaps also assumed that the 'hero's' amoral code is only seen as a nightmarish possibility, the reader is not really ever made to experience a confrontation between the two codes. At the end of the novel he feels he is really back where he started. On the other hand, the reader's expectations that decent behaviour will prevail over evil are frustrated, and the result may be a moral shock, the sort of recognition of the truth that as we have seen tends to be central in the reader's confrontation with the world of the novel.

E. M. Forster attaches great importance to the novel as including, not only a story, but also 'life by values'.[4] The inculcation of value implies the art of persuasion. All the novels examined in the present work suggest that the reader is made to undergo some kind of moral education. Based on the moral equipment he possesses initially he is enabled to respond to the moral issues raised by the novel. In the process his moral horizon and awareness are often widened so that he can cope with the new situation and fulfil his task as a moral touchstone

Emphasis on the novelist as persuader accentuates the importance of the study of point of view in fiction. The six novels offer evidence of the wide range of 'tones' which are at the novelist's disposal – relating both to mood and style and including the lofty as well as the trivial. This is perhaps particularly striking in *Brighton Rock* and *A Clockwork Orange.* Even more interesting is the way point of view is expressed through design and emphasis. In novels like *The Mayor of Casterbridge* and *A Passage to India* character and action are placed within a forever expanding framework which guides the reader's attention from man and his immediate surroundings to the infinite. Emphasis is inherent in the design itself, palpable in contour and detail, but it is above all expressed through dialogue, narrative bent, the bias given to sketches of character, metaphorical language and authorial comment. What has traditionally been associated with point of view – narrative angle – is of course a favourite means of conveying emphasis, particularly as a means of expressing the relationship between author/narrator and character/action. *A Passage to India* may serve as an example of the supreme way in which emphasis is modulated – by varying the degree of authorial presence. In *Brighton Rock,* on the other hand, the continuous presence of the authorial narrator as reporter and evaluating commentator ensures a firm framework of concepts and belief within which Pinkie's shabby little world can be outlined and given emphasis seemingly out of proportion to its 'real' dimensions. Pinkie may appear insignificant in human and social terms, but in spiritual terms he is not. For all his cruelty he acquires certain characteristics which give him universal dimensions. He is made to represent certain aspects of the human condition in the eyes of both God and man.

The dual function of character as individual and representative of mankind as a whole is often emphasized by the novelist. Through emphasis and design man is shown to transcend his limitations at certain moments and achieve universal significance. This happens to Pamela during her trials, to Silas Marner when he responds to the challenge life offers him, to Elizabeth-Jane in her lonely chamber, to such a failure as Adela in *A Passage to India* when during Dr. Aziz's trial she realizes she has been mistaken and has the courage to act accordingly. It may be a question of sudden awareness, as is clear when Pinkie is confronted with an overwhelming spiritual pressure on the day of his death. It is possible that Alex has this sort of experience when he is confronted with the treatment that will prevent him from choosing evil. Whatever their value as individual human beings, these characters are at such moments shown to transcend their normal limitations, at least for a while and to some extent.

Such moments tend to come at crucial stages in the plot and one may feel that the whole cumulative process of plot development is behind them, giving them prominence and significance. They may be watersheds in the moral development portrayed and therefore essential elements in the moral pattern of the novel. Here, too, the designer is at work, throwing moral issues into relief by arranging characters, incidents, and roles with an eye to contrast, symmetry, and exemplum.

Design is a pictorial term and can only allude to an effect the novelist can achieve by means of words. Emphasis on the other hand is a matter of verbal effect. In the last resort we have to confess that we are in the grip of words, exposed to the art of persuasion. In *The Novelist at the Crossroads* David Lodge claims that the novelist 'is committed to language all along the line . . .'[5] He makes this statement in answer to Malcolm Bradbury's suggestion that although 'all things in a fiction are mediated through words . . . certain things can be held logically and temporally antecedent to those words, as a matter which the words mediate'.[6] This Lodge considers impossible. The interest of this discussion derives partly from the fact that both critics are also practising novelists and are therefore able to view the problem from two angles.

It would seem that the student of the novelist's art of persuasion might find both views useful, perhaps in modified forms. Emphasis on the verbal nature of fiction is a reminder that the world of fiction is itself a fiction – a bundle of lies, a game of words in which the reader is meant to both recognize the lying and obey the rules of the game, which assume that the world is real.[7] At the same time the words in the novel teach the reader something – about himself, his fellow human beings, about the power of verbal art.

Bradbury's proposition, on the other hand, helps to make sense of the assumptions about reality, form and value that have been expressed in this study, and Bradbury is indeed one of the critics who takes most interest in the persuasive element in the novelist's craft:

> ... most writers would ... consider that they are making verbal approaches to a reader which would engage him with a devised reality they both might know, and that the working out of the relationships with that reader, so that he might have expectations and values, sympathies and repulsions, appropriate to that reality, is an essential part of creation.[8]

In conclusion it may be said that there is no one way of investigating the art of persuasion or the nature of the author–reader relationship. The approach should probably be empirical, in that the work itself should be in the foreground and sensitive reading on both a naive and a critical level should be a basic requirement. With this proviso any method (or combination of methods) that can throw light on the novelist's craft is welcome.

Notes

INTRODUCTION pp. 7–13

1 E. M. Forster, *Aspects of the Novel*, p. 12.
2 David Cecil, *The Fine Art of Reading*, p. 95.
3 Cf. I. A. Richard's distinction between 'the ordinary man' and the poet. *The Principles of Literary Criticism*, p. 243.
4 Cf. Malcolm Bradbury, *Possibilities*, pp. 4, 10.
5 See Alice R. Kaminsky, 'On Literary Realism', in John Halperin (ed.), *The Theory of the Novel*, p. 219.
6 See e.g. Ian Watt, *The Rise of the Novel*, pp. 9–35; W. J. Harvey, *Character and the Novel*, pp. 11–29; David Lodge, *The Novelist at the Crossroads*, pp. 3–34; George Levine, 'Realism Reconsidered' in John Halperin, *op.cit.*, pp. 233ff. See also 'Introduction' to Damian Grant, *Realism*, pp. 1–19.
7 Graham Hough, *An Essay on Criticism*, pp. 42, 44.
8 Arnold Kettle, *An Introduction to the English Novel*, vol. I, pp. 13–15.
9 Thomas Hardy, 'The Novel "An Artificiality Distilled from the Fruits of Observation"', in Miriam Allott, *Novelists on the Novel*, p. 73.
10 Barbara Hardy, *The Appropriate Form*, pp. 2–3.
11 David Lodge, *op.cit.*, p. 32.
12 Cf. John Halperin, 'The Theory of the Novel: A Critical Introduction', in John Halperin, *op.cit.*, p. 18.
13 David Lodge, *Language of Fiction*, pp. 64–5.
14 John Colmer, 'Form and Design in the Novel', in John Colmer (ed.), *Approaches to the Novel*, p. 10.
15 Wolfgang Iser, 'Indeterminacy and the Reader's Response in Prose Fiction', in J. Hillis Miller (ed.), *Aspects of Narrative*, p. 8.
16 Robert Scholes and Robert Kellogg, *The Nature of Narrative*, p. 268.
17 *Ibid.*
18 John F. Loofbourow, 'Realism in the Anglo-American Novel: The Pastoral Myth', in John Halperin, *op.cit.*, p. 260. See also David I. Grossvogel, *Limits of the Novel*, p. 18.
19 Cf. David Lodge, *loc. cit.*
20 Malcolm Bradbury, *op.cit.*, p. 290.
21 John Colmer, *op.cit.*, p. 16.
22 Wayne C. Booth, *The Rhetoric of Fiction*, 'Preface'.
23 Karl Kroeber, *Styles in Fictional Structure*, p. 43.
24 Lars Hartveit, *Dream within a Dream. A Thematic Approach to Scott's Vision of Fictional Reality*, pp. 77–102.
25 *Op.cit.*, pp. 275–292.
26 Walter F. Wright, 'Tone in Fiction', pp. 297ff.; Robert B. Heilman, 'Two-Tone Fiction: Nineteenth-Century Types and Eighteenth-Century Problems', pp. 305ff.; Walter Allen, 'Narrative Distance, Tone, and Character', pp. 323ff.

140

1 See Ch. 5, 'Love and the Novel: *Pamela*', pp. 140ff.
2 References are to the Everyman edition of *Pamela* (London, 1960).
3 Cf. M. Kinkead-Weekes, *Samuel Richardson: Dramatic Novelist*, p. 20.
4 J. Dussinger stresses the Andrews' initial importance as inculcators of 'the standards of "virtue" and "honesty" for Pamela to act upon . . .' in 'What Pamela Knew: An Interpretation', *JEGP*, vol. 69, p. 378.
5 *History of Literature in the English Language*, vol. 4, p. 245.
6 '. . . it is only when she learns to give up self-reliance and trust herself wholly to Providence, . . . to replace caution and suspicion with faith in Man as well as God . . . to have the faith to be imprudent, that she escapes from the wilderness into happiness.' M. Kinkead-Weekes, *Samuel Richardson*, p. 45.
7 See e.g. Robert Scholes and Robert Kellogg, *op.cit.*, p. 102; A. M. Kearney, 'Richardson's *Pamela*: The Aesthetic Case', in *Twentieth Century Interpretations of Pamela*, p. 79; M. Kinkead-Weekes in *History of Literature*, p. 246.
8 Ian Watt, *op.cit.* p. 174.
9 See R. F. Brissenden, 'Pamela', in *Twentieth Century Interpretations*, p. 51.
10 David Daiches, *Literary Essays*, p. 28.
11 *Ibid.*, p. 34.
12 Ian Watt, *op.cit.*, p. 199.
13 *Ibid.*, p. 200.
14 Alan Dugald McKillop, *The Early Masters of English Fiction*, p. 59.
15 See for example Ian Watt, *op.cit.*, p. 212; Frank Bradbrook, 'Samuel Richardson', in *The Pelican Guide to English Literature*, vol. 4, p. 295.
16 Alan Dugald McKillop, *op.cit.*, p. 64.
17 Ian Watt, *op.cit.*, Ch. 5, pp. 140ff.; Diana Spearman, *The Novel and Society*, pp. 50, 173ff.
18 William M. Sale, Jr., 'From *Pamela* to *Clarissa*', in R. D. Spector (ed.) *Essays on the Eighteenth Century Novel*, p. 20.
19 See also M. Kinkead-Weekes, *Samuel Richardson*, Ch. 11, pp. 462–84.
20 Cf. *ibid.*, p. 41.
21 Cf. M. A. Doody, *A Natural Passion*, p. 44.
22 Ian Watt, *op.cit.*, p. 183. 'Richardson advanced over Defoe in his heroine's ability to say no, and no again . . .' Frederick R. Karl, *A Reader's Guide to the Development of the English Novel in the 18th Century*, p. 100. See also M. A. Doody, *op.cit.*, p. 60.
23 'Though there is never . . . any attempt to minimise the duty of servants to obey their masters and know their places, yet there is a definition of the limits within which obedience should operate . . .' M. Kinkead-Weekes, *Samuel Richardson*, p. 38.
24 Ian Watt, *op.cit.*, p. 160.
25 See Rosemary Cowler, 'Introduction' to *Twentieth Century Interpretations*, pp. 8–9.
26 For the concept of the chain of being, see E. M. W. Tillyard, *The Elizabethan World Picture*, Chs. 5 and 7. The importance of this concept in the eighteenth century is shown in Basil Willey, *The Eighteenth Century Background*, pp. 47–59. The classical work on the concept is Arthur O. Lovejoy, *The Great Chain of Being*.
27 Cf. Diana Spearman, *op.cit.*, p. 219. See also M. A. Doody, *op.cit.*, pp. 15ff.
28 Carey McIntosh, 'Pamela's Clothes', in *Twentieth Century Interpretations*, p. 89.
29 Cf. also M. Kinkead-Weekes, *Samuel Richardson*, p. 66.
30 David Daiches, *op.cit.*, p. 27.
31 See Frank Bradbrook, *op.cit.*, p. 295.

32 See M. Kinkead-Weekes, *op.cit.*, pp. 47–52.

33 Sir Walter Scott, *Lives of the Novelists*, p. 229.

34 J. A. Dussinger rightly regards B.'s change as being a result of his having read Pamela's letters. *Op.cit.*, p. 386.

35 'This conviction is conveyed to the reader through Pamela's role as writer.' J. A. Dussinger, *op.cit.*, p. 394.

CHAPTER II pp. 33–49

1 See *Adam Bede*, Ch. XVII.

2 F. R. Leavis, *The Great Tradition*, p. 58.

3 R. T. Jones, *George Eliot*, p. 34.

4 Lilian Haddakin refers to 'the many juxtapositions of literal and metaphorical' in the novel. '*Silas Marner*', in Barbara Hardy (ed.) *Critical Essays on George Eliot*, p. 65.

5 All references are to the Penguin edition.

6 See A. E. S. Viner, *George Eliot*, p. 59.

7 U. C. Knoepfelmacher, *George Eliot's Early Novels. The Limits of Realism*, p. 243.

8 Cf. John Holloway, *The Victorian Sage*, p. 114.

9 'The antithesis of narrow and broad, of closed and open, recur throughout her work.' W. J. Harvey, *The Art of George Eliot*, p. 44.

10 See Q. D. Leavis's 'Introduction' to the Penguin edition of *Silas Marner*, pp. 20ff.

11 See Lilian Haddakin, *op.cit.*, p. 63.

12 See J. Holloway's discussion of the 'unhappiness' that results from Godfrey's act of rejection and the 'real happiness' that comes to Silas when his 'numb unfeeling hardness ... slowly thaws to warmer emotions of kindliness and love.' *Op.cit.*, p. 116.

13 '*Marner* is the first of her novels to take an anti-Cinderella shape ...' Q. D. Leavis, *op.cit.*, p. 34, n.

14 Barbara Hardy, *The Novels of George Eliot*, Chs. I and II.

15 *Ibid.*, p. 27.

16 See W. J. Harvey's discussion of 'dead' and 'undeveloped' metaphors in *The Art of George Eliot*, pp. 222ff.

CHAPTER III pp. 50–70

1 George Wing, *Hardy*, p. 67.

2 Irving Howe, *Thomas Hardy*, p. 96.

3 Douglas Brown, *Thomas Hardy: The Mayor of Casterbridge*, p. 15.

4 See David Cecil, *Hardy the Novelist*, p. 73.

5 J. Hillis Miller, *Thomas Hardy. Distance and Desire*, p. 7.

6 Michael Millgate, *Thomas Hardy. His Career as a Novelist*, p. 228.

7 Ian Gregor refers to the manner in which 'The authorial consciousness of the veiled narrator [is merged with] that of Elizabeth' in Ch. 24 ('the market scene'). *The Great Web. The Form of Hardy's Major Fiction*, p. 124.

8 Douglas Brown, *op.cit.*, p. 9.

9 *Ibid.*, p. 7.

10 H. C. Duffin, *Thomas Hardy*, p. 40.
11 Cf. M. Millgate, *op.cit.* p. 228.
12 All references are to the St. Martin's Library Edition, Papermac (London, 1971).
13 David Cecil, *op.cit.*, p. 28.
14 Douglas Brown, *op.cit.*, p. 59.
15 H. C. Duffin, *op.cit.*, p. 36.
16 George Wing, *op.cit.*, p. 67.
17 Northrop Frye, *Anatomy of Criticism*, p. 155.
18 G. G. Urwin, *The Mayor of Casterbridge, Notes on English Literature*, 7, pp. 48-9.
19 Cf. Ian Gregor, *op.cit.*, p. 128.
20 Cf. Roy Morell, *Thomas Hardy. The Will and the Way*, p. 12.
21 Douglas Brown, *op.cit.*, p. 36. See also Millgate on Elizabeth-Jane's role as observer, *op.cit.*, p. 228.
22 J. Hillis Miller, *op.cit.*, p. 108.
23 'The bow window that separates the banqueters at the King's Arms from the "plainer fellows . . ." also puts a stage-frame round the feast.' Jean R. Brooks, *Thomas Hardy. The Poetic Structure*, p. 200.
24 J. Hillis Miller, *op.cit.*, p. 50.
25 See Douglas Brown, *op.cit.*, p. 13.
26 Millgate writes about 'the incorporation within the structure of the novel of patterns and techniques essentially theatrical.' *Op.cit.*, p. 230.
27 J. Hillis Miller, *op.cit.*, p. 73.
28 Hardy 'conceives of his novels from an enormous height'. E. M. Forster, *op.cit.*, p. 89. See also J. R. Brooks on Hardy's 'ever-widening perspective'. *Op.cit.*, p. 140.
29 Harvey Curtis Webster, *On A Darkling Plain*, pp. 150-1.

CHAPTER IV pp. 71–94

1 E. M. Forster, *Aspects of the Novel*, p. 78.
2 Malcolm Bradbury (ed.), *E. M. Forster. A Passage to India. A Selection of Critical Essays, Casebook Series*, pp. 12, 18ff.
3 June Perry Levine, *Creation and Criticism. A Passage to India*, pp. 127-8.
4 Alan Wilde, *Art and Order. A Study of E. M. Forster*, pp. 13-14.
5 June Perry Levine, *op.cit.*, pp. 13-14.
6 All references are to the Penguin edition of *A Passage to India*.
7 The title of the novel, suggested by Whitman's poem 'Passage to India', implies a mythical/visionary approach to the world that is to be explored in the novel.
8 Frank Kermode, 'The One Orderly Product', *Casebook*, p. 218.
9 John Colmer suggests that the 'description of the trees . . . offers a momentary vision of an area of beauty midway between the squalor of Chandrapore and the sterility of the civil station'. *E. M. Forster. A Passage to India*, p. 15.
10 Alan Wilde, *op.cit.*, p. 124. The intersecting roads are reminiscent of Whitman's vision of man as pioneer: 'Lo, soul, seest thou not God's purpose from the first?/The earth to be spann'd, connected by network . . .' (*op.cit.*, stanza 2).
11 Malcolm Bradbury, 'Two Passages to India: Forster as Victorian and Modern', *Casebook*, p. 231. See also M. Bradbury, *Possibilities*, pp. 118-9.
12 Reuben A. Brower, 'The Twilight of the Double Vision: Symbol and Irony in *A Passage to India*', *Casebook*, p. 114.
13 Frederick C. Crews, 'A Passage to India', in *Casebook*, p. 172.
14 E. K. Brown takes a somewhat different view. He takes her words 'Pretty dear'

as evidence of her inclusive approach to people and setting, in contrast to the Anglo-Indian ladies, who would have been exasperated at the idea that the wasp cannot discriminate between a house and the jungle. *Rhythm in the Novel*, pp. 92–3.

15 J. B. Beer, *The Achievement of E. M. Forster*, p. 36.
16 *Ibid.*, p. 148.
17 Gertrude M. White, 'A Passage to India: Analysis and Revaluation', *Casebook*, p. 132.
18 *Ibid.*, p. 145.
19 *Ibid.*, pp. 136–7.
20 The novel approaches Forster's definition of 'prophecy' in *Aspects of the Novel*, p. 116.
21 David Shusterman, *The Quest for Certitude in E. M. Forster's Fiction*, p. 161.
22 Cf. Bradbury: 'A Passage to India is, as the Whitmanesque overtones of its title may convey, a global novel, a novel that attempts inclusively to survey mankind.' *Possibilities*, p. 111.
23 Wilfred Stone, *The Cave and the Mountain*, p. 299.
24 John Colmer, *op.cit.*, p. 39.
25 Bradbury refers to 'the physical landscape of a country which both invites meaning ... and denies any.' *Possibilities*, p. 112.
26 June Perry Levine, *op.cit.*, pp. 178–9.
27 See John Colmer, *op.cit.*, p. 43, and Wilfred Stone, *op.cit.* pp. 335–6.
28 Lionel Trilling, *E. M. Forster*, pp. 133–4.
29 Cf. Malcolm Bradbury, 'Two Passages to India ...' *Casebook*, pp. 229–30.
30 Forster detects the 'sensation of a song or of a sound' in prophetic fiction. *Aspects of the Novel*, p. 126.
31 Barbara Hardy, *The Appropriate Form*, p. 78.
32 Cf. F. R. Leavis's critical remarks on E. M. Forster's 'personal style'. *The Common Pursuit*, pp. 274–5.
33 K. W. Gransden, *E. M. Forster*, p. 101.
34 Arnold Kettle, *An Introduction to the English Novel*, vol. II, p. 163.

CHAPTER V pp. 95–116

1 Graham Greene, *Collected Essays*, p. 141.
2 David H. Hesla, 'Theological Ambiguity in the "Catholic Novels" ', in Robert O. Evans (ed.) *Graham Greene. Some Critical Considerations*, p. 103 (later refered to as *Evans*).
3 Marie-Béatrice Mesnet, *Graham Greene and the Heart of the Matter*, pp. 5, 46.
4 Kenneth Allott and Miriam Farris, *The Art of Graham Greene*, p. 15.
5 'I am a camera with its shutter open, quite passive, recording, not thinking.' Isherwood, *Goodbye to Berlin*, p. 13.
6 See Dominick P. Consolo, 'Graham Greene: Style and Stylistics in Five Novels', *Evans*, pp. 66–7.
7 All references are to the Penguin edition of *Brighton Rock*.
8 Samuel Hynes, 'Introduction' to *Graham Greene. A Collection of Critical Essays*, *Twentieth Century Views*, p. 4.
9 *Collected Essays*, p. 116.
10 A passage like this is reminiscent of Joseph Conrad, for example in *The Heart of Darkness*. Regarding Conrad's influence, see e.g. A. A. DeVitis, 'The Catholic as Novelist: Graham Greene and François Mauriac', *Evans*, pp. 121–2; Robert O. Evans, 'The Satanist Fallacy of *Brighton Rock*', *Evans*, pp. 161 (*The Heart of Darkness*).

11 The quotation is from Graham Greene, 'The Lost Childhood', *Collected Essays*, p. 18. See also Marie-Béatrice Mesnet, *op.cit.*, p. 3, and Morton Dauwen Zabel, 'The Best and the Worst', *Twentieth Century Views*, p. 39.

12 See A. Price, *Brighton Rock*, p. 98.

13 Morton Dauwen Zabel, *op.cit.*, p. 35.

14 Wayne C. Booth, *op.cit.*, p. 272.

15 See e.g. A. A. DeVitis, 'Allegory in "Brighton Rock"', *MFS*, vol. III, No. 3, pp. 216ff.; Anonymous, 'Graham Greene: The Man Within', *Twentieth Century Views*, pp. 12 ff. (legend); K. Allott and M. Farris, *op.cit.*, p. 31 (morality).

16 David Lodge, *Graham Greene*, p. 10.

17 *Ibid.*, p. 10.

18 David Pryce-Jones, *Graham Greene*, p. 32.

19 Dominick P. Consolo, *op.cit.*, *Evans*, p. 65.

20 David Lodge, *op.cit.*, p. 23.

21 Derek Traversi, 'Graham Greene: The Early Novels', *Twentieth Century Views*, p. 25.

22 A. A. DeVitis, 'Allegory in "Brighton Rock"', *MFS*, p. 217.

23 David Pryce-Jones, *op.cit.*, p. 38.

24 K. Allott and M. Farris, *op.cit.*, p. 121.

25 See *ibid.*, pp. 156–7.

26 David Lodge, *op.cit.*, p. 22.

27 'Dover Beach'.

28 Dominick P. Consolo, *op.cit.*, *Evans*, p. 64.

29 David Lodge, *Language of Fiction*, p. 50.

30 Richard Hoggart, 'The Force of Caricature', *Twentieth Century Views*, p. 86.

31 E. M. Forster uses the word 'bounce' about point of view. *Aspects of the Novel*, p. 75.

32 See Dominick P. Consolo, *op.cit.*, *Evans*, p. 71.

CHAPTER VI pp. 117–131

1 Frederick R. Karl, *A. Reader's Guide to the Contemporary English Novel*, p. 360.

2 Bernard Bergonzi, *The Situation of the Novel*, p. 216.

3 See Carol M. Dix, *Anthony Burgess*, pp. 12–13.

4 See chapter on *Brighton Rock* p. 103, above.

5 George Steiner, *Language and Silence*, p. IX.

6 All references are to the Penguin edition.

7 See A. A. DeVitis on Burgess's Manichaeanism, *Anthony Burgess*, p. 22.

8 'Ideologically, then, Burgess's point is clear: that a technologically oriented society ... in its overriding desire to change people will kill all emotion, good and bad, in the process.' Frederick R. Karl, *op.cit.*, p. 361.

9 Cf. A. A. DeVitis, *op.cit.*, pp. 104–6, 111.

10 Bernard Bergonzi, *op.cit.*, p. 217.

11 Carol M. Dix refers to Burgess's 'suspicion of our liberal humanism ...' *Op.cit.*, p. 15.

12 Frederick R. Karl, *op.cit.*, p. 361.

13 Bernard Bergonzi, *op.cit.*, p. 215.

14 Cf. A. A. DeVitis, *op.cit.*, p. 27.

15 Bernard Bergonzi, *op.cit.*, pp. 215–6.

16 Percy Lubbock, *The Craft of Fiction*, p. 140.

17 See A. A. DeVitis, *op.cit.*, p. 16.

18 Bernard Bergonzi, *op.cit.*, p. 214.

19 Cf. A. A. DeVitis, *op.cit.*, p. 105.

CONCLUSION pp. 132–139 R

1 See Peter Dixon, *Rhetoric*, p. 2.
2 David Goldknopf, *The Life of the Novel*, p. 197.
3 David Daiches, *The Novel and the Modern World*, p. 2.
4 E. M. Forster, *Aspects of the Novel*, p. 30.
5 David Lodge, *The Novelist at the Crossroads*, p. 61.
6 Malcolm Bradbury, *Possibilities*, p. 283.
7 Cf. David I. Grossvogel, *op.cit.*, p. 13; Walter F. Wright, 'Tone in Fiction', John Halperin, *op.cit.*, p. 300.
8 Malcolm Bradbury, *Possibilities*, pp. 282–3.

Bibliography

Allen, Walter, 1974. 'Narrative Distance, Tone, and Character', in *The Theory of the Novel*, see Halperin 1974.

Allott, Kenneth and Miriam Farris, 1963. *The Art of Graham Greene*, New York.

Allott, Miriam, 1966. *Novelists on the Novel*, New York.

Anonymous, 'Graham Greene: The Man Within', in *Graham Greene. A Collection of Critical Essays, Twentieth Century Views*, see Hynes 1973.

Beer, John Bernard, 1962. *The Achievement of E. M. Forster*, London.

Bergonzi, Bernard, 1972. *The Situation of the Novel*, Harmondsworth.

Booth, Wayne, C., 1967. *The Rhetoric of Fiction*, Chicago.

Bradbrook, Frank, 1972. 'Samuel Richardson', in *The Pelican Guide to English Literature*, see Ford 1972.

Bradbury, Malcolm, (ed.), 1970. *E. M. Forster. A Passage to India. A Selection of Critical Essays. Casebook,* London.

Bradbury, Malcolm, 'Introduction', *Casebook.*

Bradbury, Malcolm, 'Two Passages to India', *Casebook.*

Bradbury, Malcolm, 1973. *Possibilities,* London.

Brissenden, R. F., 1969. 'Pamela', in *Twentieth Century Interpretations of Pamela,* see Cowler 1969.

Brooks, Jean R., 1971. *Thomas Hardy. The Poetic Structure,* London.

Brower, Reuben A., 1970. 'The Twilight of the Double Vision: Symbol and Irony in *A Passage to India*', *Casebook,* see Bradbury, 1970.

Brown, Douglas, 1962. *Thomas Hardy: The Mayor of Casterbridge, Studies in English Literature,* No. 7, London.

Brown, E. K., 1963. *Rhythm in the Novel,* Toronto.

Cecil, Lord David, 1957. *The Fine Art of Reading,* London.

Cecil, Lord David, 1954. *Hardy the Novelist,* London.

Colmer, John (ed.), 1967. *Approaches to the Novel,* London.

Colmer, John, 1969. *E. M. Forster. A Passage to India, Studies in English Literature,* No. 30, London.

Colmer, John, 1967. 'Form and Design in the Novel', in *Approaches to the Novel,* see Colmer 1967.

Consolo, Dominich P., 1963. 'Graham Greene: Style and Stylistics in Five Novels', in *Graham Greene. Some Critical Considerations,* see Evans 1963.

Cowler, Rosemary (ed.), 1969. *Twentieth Century Interpretations of Pamela,* Englewood Cliffs, N.J.

Cowler, Rosemary, 'Introduction' to *Twentieth Century Interpretations of Pamela.*

Crews, Frederick C., 1970. 'A Passage to India', *Casebook,* see Bradbury 1970.

Daiches, David, 1956. *Literary Essays,* Edinburgh.

Daiches, David, 1965. *The Novel and the Modern World,* Chicago.

DeVitis, A. A., 1957. 'Allegory in "Brighton Rock" ', *MFS,* Vol. III, No. 3.

DeVitis, A. A., 1972. *Anthony Burgess,* New York.

DeVitis, A. A., 1963. 'The Catholic as Novelist: Graham Greene and François Mauriac', in *Graham Greene. Some Critical Considerations,* see Evans 1963.

Dix, Carol M., 1971. *Anthony Burgess, Writers and their Work,* London.

Dixon, Peter, 1971. *Rhetoric,* London.

Doody, Margaret Anne, 1974. *A Natural Passion. A Study of the Novels of Samuel Richardson,* Oxford.

Duffin, Henry Charles, 1962. *Thomas Hardy,* Manchester.

Dussinger, John A., 1970. 'What Pamela Knew: An Interpretation', *JEGP,* Vol. 69.

Evans, Robert O. (ed.), 1963. *Graham Greene. Some Critical Considerations,* University of Kentucky Press.

Evans, Robert O., 'The Satanist Fallacy of Brighton Rock', in *Graham Greene. Some Critical Considerations.*

Ford, Boris (ed.), 1972. *The Pelican Guide to English Literature,* Vol. IV, Harmondsworth.

Forster, E. M., 1958. *Aspects of the Novel,* London.

Frye, Northrop, 1966. *Anatomy of Criticism,* New York.

Goldknopf, David, 1972. *The Life of the Novel,* Chicago.

Gransden, K. W., 1962. *E. M. Forster,* Edinburgh.

Grant, Damian, 1970. *Realism,* London.

Greene, Graham, 1969. *Collected Essays,* London.

Gregor, Ian, 1974. *The Great Web. The Form of Hardy's Major Fiction,* London.

Grossvogel, David I., 1968. *Limits of the Novel,* Ithaca, N.Y.

Haddakin, Lilian, 1970. 'Silas Marner', in *Critical Essays on George Eliot,* see Hardy 1970.

Halperin, John (ed.), 1974. *The Theory of the Novel,* New York.

Halperin, John, 'The Theory of the Novel: A Critical Introduction', in *The Theory of the Novel.*

Hardy, Barbara, 1959. *The Novels of George Eliot,* London.

Hardy, Barbara (ed.), 1970. *Critical Essays on George Eliot,* London.

Hardy, Barbara, 1971. *The Appropriate Form,* London.

Hartveit, Lars, 1974. *Dream within a Dream. A Thematic Approach to Scott's Vision of Fictional Reality,* Bergen.

Harvey, W. J., 1963. *The Art of George Eliot,* London.

Harvey, W. J., 1966. *Character and the Novel,* London.

Heilman, Robert B., 1974. 'Two-Tone Fiction: Nineteenth-Century Types and Eighteenth-Century Problems', in *The Theory of the Novel,* see Halperin 1974.

Hesla, David H., 1963. 'Theological Ambiguity in the "Catholic Novels" ', in *Graham Greene. Some Critical Considerations,* see Evans 1963.

Hoggart, Richard, 1973. 'The Force of Caricature', in *Twentieth Century Views,* see Hynes 1973.

Holloway, John, 1962. *The Victorian Sage,* London.

Hough, Graham, 1966. *An Essay on Criticism,* London.

Howe, Irving, 1968. *Thomas Hardy,* London.

Hynes, Samuel (ed.), 1973. *Graham Greene. A Collection of Critical Essays. Twentieth Century Views,* Englewood Cliffs, N.J.

Hynes, Samuel, 'Introduction', in *Twentieth Century Views.*

Iser, Wolfgang, 1971. 'Indeterminacy and the Reader's Response in Prose Fiction' in *Aspects of Narrative,* see Miller 1971.

Isherwood, Christopher, 1969. *Goodbye to Berlin,* London.

Jones, T. R., 1970. *George Eliot,* Cambridge.

Kaminsky, Alice R., 1974. 'On Literary Realism', in *The Theory of the Novel,* see Halperin 1974.

Karl, Frederick R., 1972. *A Reader's Guide to the Contemporary English Novel,* New York.

Karl, Frederick R., 1975. *A Reader's Guide to the Development of the English Novel in the Eighteenth Century,* London.

Kearney, A. M., 1969. 'Richardson's *Pamela*: The Aesthetic Case', in *Twentieth Century Interpretations of Pamela,* see Cowler 1969.

Kermode, Frank, 1970. 'The One Orderly Product', *Casebook,* see Bradbury 1970.

Kettle, Arnold, 1957. *An Introduction to the English Novel,* London.

Kinkead-Weekes, Mark, 1973. *Samuel Richardson: Dramatic Novelist,* London.

Knoepfelmacher, Ulrich Camillus, 1968. *George Eliot's Early Novels. The Limits of Realism,* Berkeley and Los Angeles.

Kroeber, Karl, 1971. *Styles in Fictional Structure,* Princeton, N.J.

Leavis, F. R., 1952. *The Common Pursuit,* Harmondsworth.

Leavis, F. R., 1962. *The Great Tradition,* Harmondsworth.

Leavis, Q. D., 1967. 'Introduction' to *Silas Marner,* Harmondsworth.

Levine, George, 1974. 'Realism Reconsidered', in *The Theory of the Novel,* see Halperin 1974.

Levine, June Perry, 1971. *Creation and Criticism. A Passage to India,* London.

Lodge, David, 1966. *Graham Greene, Columbia Essays on Modern Writers,* No. 17, New York.

Lodge, David, 1967. *Language of Fiction,* New York.

Lodge, David, 1971. *The Novelist at the Crossroads,* London.

Lonsdale, Roger (ed.), 1971. *History of Literature in the English Language,* Vol. IV, London.

Loofbourow, John F., 1974. 'Realism in the Anglo-American Novel: The Pastoral Myth', in *The Theory of the Novel,* see Halperin 1974.

Lovejoy, Arthur O., 1957. *The Great Chain of Being. A Study of the History of an Idea,* Cambridge, Mass.

Lubbock, Percy, 1957. *The Craft of Fiction,* London.

McIntosh, Carey, 1969. 'Pamela's Clothes', in *Twentieth Century Interpretations of Pamela,* see Cowler 1969.

McKillop, Alan Dugald, 1968. *The Early Masters of English Fiction,* Lawrence, Kansas.

Mesnet, Marie-Béatrice, 1954, *Graham Greene and the Heart of the Matter,* London.

Miller, J. Hillis (ed.), 1971. *Aspects of Narrative,* New York.

Miller, J. Hillis, 1970. *Thomas Hardy. Distance and Desire,* Cambridge, Mass.

Millgate, Michael, 1971. *Thomas Hardy. His Career as a Novelist,* London.

Morrell, Roy, 1968. *Thomas Hardy. The Will and the Way,* Singapore.

Price, Alan, 1969. *Brighton Rock, Notes on English Literature,* No. 40, Oxford.

Pryce-Jones, David, 1963, *Graham Greene,* Edinburgh.

Richards, Ivor A., 1947. *Principles of Literary Criticism,* London.

Sale, William M., Jr., 1965. 'From *Pamela* to *Clarissa*', in *Essays on the Eighteenth Century Novel,* see Spector 1965.

Scholes, Robert and Robert Kellogg, 1968. *The Nature of Narrative,* New York.

Scott, Sir Walter, 1934. *Lives of the Novelists,* London.

Shusterman, David, 1965. *The Quest for Certitude in E. M. Forster's Fiction,* Bloomington, Indiana.

Spearman, Diana, 1966. *The Novel and Society,* London.

Spector, Robert D. (ed.), 1965. *Essays on the Eighteenth Century Novel,* Bloomington, Ind.

Steiner, George, 1970. *Language and Silence,* New York.

Stone, Wilfred, 1966. *The Cave and the Mountain,* Stanford, Calif.

Tillyard, E. M. W., 1963. *The Elizabethan World Picture,* Harmondsworth.

Traversi, Derek, 1973. 'Graham Greene: The Early Novels', in *Twentieth Century Views,* see Hynes 1973.

Trilling, Lionel, 1967. *E. M. Forster,* London.

Urwin, Georg Glencairn, 1964. *The Mayor of Casterbridge, Notes on English Literature,* No. 7, Oxford.
Viner, A. E. S., 1971. *George Eliot,* Edinburgh.
Watt, Ian, 1963. *The Rise of the Novel,* Harmondsworth.
Webster, Harvey Curtis, 1947. *On a Darkling Plain,* Chicago.
White, Gertrude M., 1970. 'A Passage to India: Analysis and Revaluation', in *Casebook,* see Bradbury 1970.
Wilde, Alan, 1965. *Art and Order. A Study of E. M. Forster,* London.
Willey, Basil, 1962. *The Eighteenth Century Background,* Harmondsworth.
Wing, George, 1963. *Hardy,* Edinburgh.
Wright, Walter F., 1974. 'Tone in Fiction', in *The Theory of the Novel,* see Halperin 1974.
Zabel, Morton Dauwen, 1973. 'The Best and the Worst', in *Twentieth Century Views,* see Hynes 1973.

Index